Botany on Your Plate

Investigating the Plants We Eat

Katharine D. Barrett

Jennifer M. White

Christine Manoux

Published by
the National Gardening Association
Burlington, Vermont

University of California Botanical Garden
200 Centennial Drive, Berkeley, CA 94720-5045
Director: Paul Licht

The University of California Botanical Garden at Berkeley is a living museum open to the public featuring one of the most diverse plant collections in the United States, and extensive education and outreach programs serving schools and community groups throughout California and the nation. Established in 1890, the Garden's 34 acres contain over 12,000 taxa and more than 9,000 species from all over the world arranged by region. The mission of the Garden is to develop and maintain a diverse living collection of plants to support teaching and worldwide research in plant biology, further the conservation of plant diversity, and promote public understanding and appreciation of plants and the natural environment.
http://botanicalgarden.berkeley.edu

HHMI **The Howard Hughes Medical Institute** provided funding to the UC Botanical Garden in 1997 to develop materials that promote science investigations connected to school garden programs. A second cycle of funding in 2001 enabled project leaders to further develop and test added connections to literacy, nutrition, and mathematics.

Shasta Wildlife Conservation Foundation

Additional support was provided by the **National Science Foundation** and the **Shasta Wildlife Conservation Foundation.** This funding does not necessarily imply endorsement of *Botany on Your Plate* or responsibility for statements or views expressed in this publication.

Botanical information and most of the graphic images in the Botany Background section are from *The California Master Gardener Handbook,* 2004 edition, and are used by permission of the publisher, the University of California Agriculture and Natural Resources. This books and other publications are available for purchase at *http://anrcatalog.ucdavis.edu.*

National Gardening Association
1100 Dorset Street, South Burlington, Vermont 05403
(802) 863-5251
President: Michael C. Metallo

Founded in 1973, the **National Gardening Association** (NGA) is a nonprofit organization dedicated to promoting home, school, and community gardening as a means to renewing and sustaining the essential connection between people, plants, and the environment. NGA's programs and initiatives highlight opportunities for plant-based education in schools, communities, and backyards across the country and connect people to gardening in five core fields: plant-based education, health and wellness, environmental stewardship, community development, and responsible home gardening. *www.garden.org*

ISBN-13: 978-0-915873-49-4

Library of Congress Control Number: 2007942228

Dedication

This curriculum is dedicated to the Docents of the UC Botanical Garden in appreciation for their more than 30 years of teaching and inspiring the next generation to love plants.

Project Staff

AUTHORS
Katharine D. Barrett
Jennifer M. White
Christine Manoux

EDITOR
Christine Manoux

GRAPHIC DESIGN & LAYOUT
Alison Watt

LESSON DIAGRAMS
Jennifer M. White
Alex Moquist (p. 67)

COLOR ILLUSTRATIONS
Ann Williams

PHOTOGRAPHY
Jennifer M. White
Christine Manoux
Wade Barrett

Curriculum Development Advisors

UC BOTANICAL GARDEN PROGRAMS

Staff: Chris Carmichael, Holly Forbes

UC Berkeley faculty: Lewis Feldman, Robert Raabe

Graduate students: Jeff Obirek, Darissa Phipps, Joshua Povich

Lawrence Hall of Science: Mary Connolly, Heidi Schnabel, Joanna Totino

Howard Hughes Medical Institute advisors

HAYWARD UNIFIED SCHOOL DISTRICT

Nutritional Learning Community Program: Christine Boynton

Teachers: Carolyn Bates, Kate Day, Jeannie Greiner, Joanna Katz

Kids Breakfast Club: Marlena Urik

Adult English for Special Purposes: Phil Roche

Spanish translation: Araceli Curiel, Richard Meux

BERKELEY UNIFIED SCHOOL DISTRICT

Teachers: Susan Alexander, Rita Davies, Katie Johnson, Cathy Jones, Laurie Nielson, Amy Norris, Jackie Omania, Mary Raguth, Kathleen Richerson

Principal: Kathleen Lewis

Garden educator: Rivka Mason

OAKLAND UNIFIED SCHOOL DISTRICT

Teachers: Isabel Padilla, Bonnie Riner, Sonia Rodriguez, Joanna Schiller, Severin Siverson

Principals: Geraldine Camacho, Roberta Teller

WEST CONTRA COSTA UNIFIED SCHOOL DISTRICT

Teacher: Peter Perrault

INFORMAL EDUCATION YOUTH PROGRAMS

SF Bay Area Girl Scout Council
Atlanta Botanical Garden
Brooklyn Botanical Garden
Chicago Botanic Garden
Missouri Botanical Garden
Morris Arboretum
UC Davis Arboretum
Florida Science Center
Houston Children's Museum
4-H California
Jacoba Van Staveren

Acknowledgements

Much as plant growth is the result of numerous processes and resources coming together, the development of this unit has brought together the expertise of teachers, scientists, parent volunteers, and community leaders to engage children in investigating the interactions between plants, people, and the environment. The idea for *Botany on Your Plate* first grew out of the UC Botanical Garden's successful 25-year-old, docent-led presentation titled "Grocery Store Botany." Using the foods we eat to teach botany, this one-hour in-class program, based on Myrtle Wolf's master's thesis, overseen by U.C. Botany Professor Dr. Herbert Mason, was developed and has been presented to thousands of East Bay elementary students by UCBG Docents Elly Bade, Linda Govan, Nancy Markell, Mary Pierpont, Cyndy Plambeck, Jane Sandstrom, Sandy Sobey, Lynn Winter, Jacquline Woodfill, and Florence Yaffe.

Through grant funding, *Botany on Your Plate* became a multi-lesson series. The project has worked with more than 20 schools and 100 teachers in four San Francisco East Bay school districts, testing the activities with children in grades K-6. Youth educators in school and botanical garden programs across the country also provided informal testing. Beginning in 2004, the Hayward Unified School District's Nutritional Learning Communities Program provided leadership and classroom support to trial the curriculum in more than 10 schools. Combined feedback from youth educators and teachers contributed to refining activities for age-appropriate concepts supporting Standards for science, mathematics, language arts, social studies, and nutrition.

Effectiveness Study

Early in 2005, two students from the UC Berkeley Graduate School of Education, Darissa Phipps and Jeff Oberik, conducted an evaluation study of *Botany on Your Plate* in three schools in the Hayward Unified School District. The study was exploratory in nature and focused on changes in science content knowledge and attitudes towards fruits and vegetables for children in grades K-3. The pre- and post-data collected showed significant success in target outcomes. Following the *Botany on Your Plate* curriculum intervention, 95 percent of the student population assessed reported that they seek out and eat more fruits and vegetables when making choices for their diet. Per grade level, results were similar.

Kindergarten students showed strong gains in understanding that plant sources provide food, and 89 percent reported greater preference for eating fruits and vegetables. Ninety-three percent of first grade students reported the same, as did 90 percent of the second grade students. All third grade students reported a greater preference for increasing their consumption of fruits and vegetables following completion of the curriculum. Students also demonstrated gains in knowledge regarding plant parts and their respective functions: 85 percent of the students increased their identification knowledge of basic plant parts, and 78 percent responded with greater ability to identify part functions.

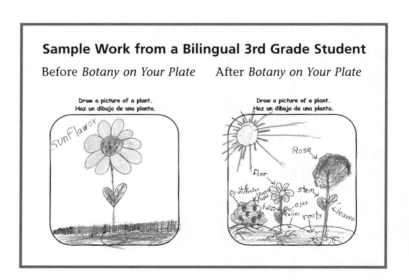

Sample Work from a Bilingual 3rd Grade Student

Before *Botany on Your Plate*   After *Botany on Your Plate*

Table of Contents

Introduction

Welcome to *Botany on Your Plate,* a life science unit for grades K-4 that inspires children to explore the fascinating realm of plants we eat. Every lesson begins with plant tastings that spark curiosity, interesting questions, and social dialogue to fuel the learning process. This inquiry approach engages children as botanists observing and collecting data, discussing findings, and reflecting on what they learn as they study edible roots, stems, leaves, flowers, fruits, and seeds. Many schools have adopted the curriculum because it weaves nutritional health, mathematics, language arts, and social studies together with investigative science.

The lessons in *Botany on Your Plate* are valuable for all ages. You can modify how students document their work or the extent of vocabulary you use to match the skill level of your group. For example, have pre-literate students document their work through drawings and older students write descriptive paragraphs. You can also simplify or extend these lessons by choosing the amount and sophistication of science content, math, and language arts to best suit your children.

Children Apply Investigative Skills

Long ago people around the world began using the processes of science and mathematics to investigate the characteristics of plants. These early botanists compared the structures of plants and selectively propagated the ones best suited for foods and materials. Every culture measured, evaluated, and celebrated the harvest. Your students will estimate number of seeds, predict the movement of water, compare structures, analyze food preference data, and diagram their findings.

Children Become Food Explorers

The health of our children depends on a diet rich in whole plant foods. Exploring and tasting fresh produce is a central theme of *Botany on Your Plate.* Research shows that repeated exposures to a new food often lead people to add the item to their general diet. Each investigation begins with plant snacks that entail sensory comparisons and discussions. Children learn about the nutrient values of various plant parts while savoring their flavors, aromas, and textures. You will likely find that some food plants will be familiar to several of your students and yet exotic to others. *Botany on Your Plate* provides the opportunity to celebrate the rich cultures represented in your classroom through plants and foods. We urge you to encourage open-mindedness in your children as they eat and describe foods from the gardens of the world.

Children Communicate Observations and Ideas

Watching a butterfly emerge may be a single life-changing experience for a person, but it is the detailed documentation and sharing of the observation that brings it into the scientific process. Carefully recorded observations provide stepping-stones for other scientists to evaluate, revisit, and build upon past events and findings. Children develop and hone their evidence-gathering skills while investigating edible plants and documenting their observations in their journals. They are challenged to consider alternate explanations and to identify new questions for study. Working in pairs, they record and talk about the plant  structures they are dissecting and drawing. They contribute findings to the group discussion, and as individuals they reflect on what they have learned and topics that pique their curiosity. The rich scientific content and collaborative social process promotes language acquisition and development of oral and written communication skills, and each chapter includes language arts activities.

Children Learn Important Skills and Knowledge Across Disciplines

This unit provides strong support to major learning goals outlined in the National Science Education Standards. The sessions interweave life science with environmental science and connect strongly to the "science and inquiry" standards. *Botany on Your Plate* was further designed to support mathematics, language arts, and social studies standards, as well as health standards related to nutrition. At the end of every lesson are Going Further activities in multiple subject areas. Teachers have also extended the curriculum's use of botanical drawing to teach art. The highly sensorial and experiential nature of the lessons engages all learners, enriching their understanding and thinking across subject areas. This is especially true with English Language Learners.

Children Apply What They Learn to Cooking and Gardening

As children discover new foods and learn to dissect fruits and vegetables safely, their parents report a parallel interest in helping to shop for produce and prepare healthy meals at home. *Botany on Your Plate* was developed in collaboration with teachers, parents, and youth educators. Moms, dads, and grandparents attending classes for English as a Second Language have taken activities home to involve their youngsters in cooking and gardening. Garden educators, volunteers, and teachers who are part of the national school garden movement have used this unit to link planting and harvesting activities with their programs and the classroom. Food service personnel at partner schools have played an important role in supporting class-room investigations with lunchroom salad bars and fresh fruit and vegetable choices. We encourage you to build a community of collaborators to broaden and deepen the ways children apply this new appreciation of edible plants to their everyday lives!

Active Assessment and Standards-Based Learning Outcomes

How do we know that children are learning what we want them to learn? Assessment is an important tool for enabling educators to adapt and modify their programs to the changing needs of students and the changing goals of our educational systems. Ultimately, we want students to become evaluators of their own learning and to have the curiosity and motivation to continue investigating the world around them. We want them to become life-long learners who actively seek knowledge and skills.

The goal of productive assessment is twofold: (1) to recognize student progress and illuminate needs for future growth; and (2) to guide adults in stimulating and empowering each child to achieve his or her full learning potential. Curiosity, persistence, critical thinking, and communicating ideas are among behaviors that indicate children are enjoying the process of learning. As you progress through *Botany on Your Plate* activities, look for the following kinds of behaviors as evidence that learning is taking place: journal writing, use of new vocabulary, drawings and diagrams, helping other children, correcting incorrect information, sharing information in class discussions, using equipment to measure and observe, recognition of something learned, using new knowledge in a new circumstance, bringing in their own knowledge to make comparisons, and spending time investigating and seeking more information.

Pre-Evaluating Student Knowledge and Attitudes
Student responses that you collect in charts and journals during Lesson 1 provide baseline information about the interests, fears, skills, and knowledge that children bring to the activity.

Post-Evaluating Student Knowledge and Attitudes
At the end of the unit, revisit the Food Preference Study data and other charts and ask students to add new information to the charts. They will benefit from a second and deeper analysis of the snack data. During a final session of reflective journal writing, include students in the assessment process by asking each child to analyze and critique his or her own learning from the unit.

Botany Journal
These notebooks are excellent vehicles for assessment, and can reveal the progression of student learning and understanding. Throughout the unit, students document their observations with writing and diagrams. They also reflect upon the importance of what they have learned and suggest possible applications to new situations.

Classroom Discussions

In each of the sessions, you will guide group discussions that draw forth students' observations, questions, and predictions. These exchanges provide important opportunities for you to gauge students' concept acquisition and reasoning, as well as growth of communication skills.

Reflective Stories

Story writing is a creative opportunity for children to show what they have learned. For example, students can create a story involving a plant they have observed during the lessons. Provide guidelines for these storytelling efforts by requiring that students include 5 to 10 direct observations of plant characteristics.

Home Studies

Encourage students to conduct an investigation at home with their family and report the findings during a class presentation. These projects might include a plant food preference study, an experiment with how water travels through a plant, and a seed germination investigation.

Learning Outcomes Based on Standards

This unit provides strong support for major content standards outlined in the National Academy of Sciences, National Standards for Science Education, and by the National Council of Teachers of Mathematics (NCTM) Principals and Standards of School Mathematics. The activities interweave life science with environmental science and support science as inquiry. *Botany on Your Plate* was also designed to support certain language arts and social studies standards, as well as health education goals related to nutrition.

Students improve their inquiry skills in science and mathematics, as they:

✳ Improve their skills for making careful observations and depicting observations accurately through scale drawings, writing, and class discussions.

✳ Deepen their understanding of number, operation, and statistics through estimating, recording, counting, ordering, comparing, and analyzing data.

✳ Develop measurement concepts and skills through measuring length, area, volume, and weight using nonstandard and standard units.

✳ Pose questions and hypotheses to investigate.

✳ Use evidence to draw conclusions and critique conclusions.

Students increase their content knowledge of life science, as they:

✳ Describe the role of plants in supporting life on earth.

✳ Demonstrate their knowledge of the flowering plant's life cycle through careful dissection and diagrams, and written and oral presentations.

* Generalize their knowledge of plant characteristics and needs by identifying structures and functions in new plant examples.

* Identify and document structural patterns and symmetry in plants.

* Increase their knowledge of the diversity of plants and plants' relationships to the environment.

Students develop an understanding and appreciation of the role of plants in human health and the environment, as they:

* Experience new plant foods and increase the variety of plant foods they eat.

* Develop responsible behaviors for preparing and eating plant foods.

* Identify several ways that plants are important to humans, other animals, and the environment.

* Identify factors influencing what plant foods people eat, and demonstrate their appreciation of the health benefits of eating plants.

* Demonstrate their appreciation for the cultural diversity of foods and recipes.

Students develop an understanding of science as a human endeavor, as they:

* Describe ways that farmers and botanists in cultures around the world have influenced how we use plants for food.

* Gain skill in reporting their own scientific investigations and findings by documenting observations and evidence in their journals and class discussions.

* Describe experiments that scientists have conducted to reveal the mysteries of plant functions.

* Describe jobs and professions related to botany.

* Connect the history of plants and people with present relationships between plants, human cultures, and the environment.

Students develop skills for communicating their ideas and observations, as they:

* Write brief expository descriptions of observed plant structures and functions, using sensory details.

* Write clear sentences and paragraphs that develop a central idea or story about plants and their pollinators.

* Ask questions for clarification and understanding.

* Deliver brief oral presentations about plant investigations.

* Listen critically and respond appropriately to oral communication.

Master List of Supplies and Produce

The following supplies support the sequence of lessons delving into the six major parts of flowering plants. Quantities are based on the standard size of primary school classrooms: 20 students, plus two extras for the teacher and for demonstrations. The activities are designed for children to work with a partner or in a group of four. This master list can assist with planning and shopping. Each lesson also includes a complete list of supplies.

We suggest you assemble a **Plant Products Kit** containing several preserved and nonperishable examples of commercial uses for each plant part. Many plant parts are dried for food, seasonings, and tea. Ask friends to save washed, labeled containers from olives, artichoke hearts, and other preserved plants. If you label these and cluster them by plant part in zipper-locking plastic bags, several classes can share one kit.

Whenever possible, purchase or harvest organic produce for the snacks and dissections in these lessons. Include an example of the entire plant, such as a carrot or a radish, leaves and all. Purchase or harvest produce no more than a day or two before the lesson so it is at its best for students to observe and eat. The **Produce Shopping List by Lesson** enumerates items needed on a lesson-by-lesson basis. It is important to use the specific items listed for student investigations. However, you can modify the plant snack and additional suggested items, depending on what is available or in season in your area. Remember to choose examples of produce used by the different cultural heritages of your students. Consider saving and reusing items in multiple lessons, such as the head of lettuce with fibrous roots in the leaf lesson or a fruit with edible seeds in the seed lesson.

General Supplies

For snacks
* sink or dish pan
* dishwashing liquid
* large kitchen knife for preparing snacks and demonstrations
* 10-12 containers (medium bowls or trays)
* cutting board
* 12 serving spoons or tongs
* paper plates
* paper napkins
* roll of paper towels
* instant hand sanitizing gel (optional)

For students
(20-24 students working in pairs)
* 12 cutting boards (or plates)
* 12 inexpensive, nonserrated paring knives
* 12 hand lenses
* 12 sturdy metal spoons for seed "squash"
* pencils
* crayons or colored pencils
* student journals

continued on page 12

General Supplies, continued

For the group

- ❋ overhead transparencies or tabloid-size copies of diagrams and charts:
  - – Structures of a Tomato Plant diagram
  - – Photosynthesis diagram
  - – Parts of a Nasturtium Flower diagram
  - – Inside a Fava Bean diagram
  - – Inside an Almond Seed diagram
- ❋ chart paper for creating these charts:
  - – What Plants Do I Eat
  - – How Do People Use Plants
  - – What Fruits and Vegetables Do I Eat
- ❋ flower pollinator puppets (if you don't have finger puppets, tape a picture of each pollinator — hummingbird, bee, bat, butterfly, moth, beetle, fly — to the end of a pencil)
- ❋ flower models — enlarge the Parts of a Flower diagram or use large paper models with stamens, pollen, and a prominent stigma on the pistil
- ❋ box of flat toothpicks
- ❋ food coloring — red and blue
- ❋ tape
- ❋ 11"x 2" paper sentence strips
- ❋ marking pens

Plant Products Kit *(Choose dry or packaged examples for each plant part. The following suggestions can get you started.)*

- ❋ zip-locking bags or storage containers

Roots
- ❋ tapioca (cassava root)
- ❋ horseradish

Stems
- ❋ aspirin (originally made from willow)
- ❋ bamboo (stake, cutting board, utensil)
- ❋ cork
- ❋ maple syrup
- ❋ rubber bands
- ❋ wood (paper, pencil, toy)
- ❋ sugar (cane)
- ❋ cinnamon sticks

Leaves
- ❋ bay leaves
- ❋ garlic
- ❋ seasonings (rosemary, tarragon)
- ❋ tea

Flowers
- ❋ candied violets
- ❋ canned artichoke hearts
- ❋ packaged daylilies (available at most Asian markets)
- ❋ tea (chamomile, hibiscus, jasmine, rose petal)

Fruits
- ❋ dried chilies
- ❋ cucumber pickles
- ❋ banana chips
- ❋ allspice berries
- ❋ raisins
- ❋ vanilla bean

Seeds
- ❋ chocolate and cocoa beans or nibs
- ❋ coconut
- ❋ coffee beans
- ❋ grains (barley, corn, oats, rice, wheat)
- ❋ legumes (beans, lentils, peanuts, peas, soy)
- ❋ nuts (cashews, pecans, pinenuts)
- ❋ seeds (poppy, pumpkin, sesame, sunflower)

Produce Shopping List by Lesson *(for 20-24 students)*

Lesson 1: Let's Be Botanists!

✳ plant snack items (4 cut pieces of each item/child)
  – carrots or jicama
  – asparagus, kohlrabi, or broccoli stems
  – celery, red cabbage, or spinach
  – broccoli florets, cauliflower, or nasturtium
  – red bell pepper slices, cucumbers, tomatoes, or raisins
  – almonds or fresh beans (out of pod)

Lesson 2: Roots

✳ plant snack items (cut into pieces)
  – 1 large jicama, peeled
  – 5-6 carrots for carrot sticks
  – 4-6 radishes to cut into slices

✳ investigation items
  – 12 radishes — large, with leaves and obvious root hairs
  – butterhead lettuce or wheat grass with fibrous roots

✳ additional suggested items
  – carrot with leaves attached
  – beet with tops
  – daikon
  – parsnip
  – turnip
  – sweet potato or yam

Lesson 3: Stems

Note: Purchase the asparagus that will be used for dissection ahead of time and place the spears in blue food coloring a day before the activity so the stems have plenty of time to absorb the dye.

✳ plant snack items (cut into pieces)
  – 6-7 asparagus spears cut into sticks
  – 2-4 kohlrabi or 3 broccoli stems

✳ investigation items
  – 12 asparagus spears
  – 4-6 aging potatoes with "sprouting eyes"
  – Nopales (cactus) pad
  – white Gerber daisy
  – mint, basil, or other plant with a series of leaf nodes on its stems

✳ additional suggested items
  – potatoes (russet, red, blue)
  – sugar cane
  – bamboo shoots
  – ginger (rhizome)

Lesson 4: Leaves

Note: Purchase the celery that will be used for dissection ahead of time and place the stalks in blue food coloring a day before the activity.

✳ plant snack items (cut into pieces)
 – 1 large bunch of celery with leaves attached and, if possible, roots (save half for the demonstration)
 – 1 small head of red cabbage

✳ investigation items
 – 24 mint leaves
 – 24 leafy celery stalks

✳ additional suggested items
 – spinach
 – fresh herbs (cilantro, basil)

 – collard greens
 – chard or kale
 – green onion or leek
 – romaine lettuce
 – bok choy
 – rhubarb (leaf petiole)

Lesson 5: Flowers

✳ plant snack items (cut into pieces)
 – 1 small head cauliflower
 – 4-5 broccoli crowns

✳ investigation items
 – 24 simple flowers (nasturtiums, vinca, primrose, or alstroemeria)

✳ additional suggested items
 – artichokes
 – broccoflower or romanesco (hybrid cross of broccoli and cauliflower)
 – edible, pesticide-free flowers (pansies, squash blossoms, roses, banana flowers, borage, calendula)

Lesson 6: Fruits

✳ plant snack items (cut into pieces)
 – 4 red bell peppers
 – 1 green bell pepper
 – basket of cherry tomatoes
 – bag of grapes

✳ investigation items
 – 24 cherry tomatoes*
 – 24 globe grapes* with seeds
 Note: Tomatoes and grapes should be about the same size.

– 1 large tomato for demonstration

✳ additional suggested items
 – apple
 – banana
 – melon
 – orange
 – pea or bean pods

– pomegranate
– squash (different summer and winter varieties)
– cucumber
– blueberries, blackberries, or other cane berries

Lesson 7: Seeds

✳ plant snack items (cut into pieces)
 – bag of almonds or sunflower seeds
 – 1-2 containers of hummus (chickpea spread)
 – 1 loaf of whole-grain bread with seeds

✳ investigation items
 – 24 raw almonds
 – 24 fava or lima beans

✳ additional suggested items
 – fresh soy beans (edamame)
 – peas (in pods)
 – shelled nuts (pinenuts, pecans)
 – sunflower seeds

Lesson 8: Plants—Top to Bottom

✳ plant snack items (4 cut pieces of each item/child)
 – carrots or jicama
 – asparagus, kohlrabi, or broccoli stems
 – celery, red cabbage, or spinach

– broccoli florets, cauliflower, or nasturtiums
– red bell pepper slices, cucumbers, tomatoes, or raisins
– almonds or fresh beans (out of pod)

Let's Become Botanists!

Welcome students into the tradition of plant science — botany — which is practiced by all cultures. As botanists, students will investigate and document the amazing structures and processes of plants, while also tasting and comparing edible plants. This lesson establishes the protocols of the unit, documents prior knowledge, and creates a record of the children's plant food choices.

During a pre-assessment discussion, invite children to share what they know about the uses of plants and the kinds of plants they commonly eat. List their ideas on charts, and revisit these charts in future lessons to add new information. Children will also record their observations and data in a journal, which becomes an important document for assessing knowledge and skills.

Throughout human history botanists have studied edible plants. Children will share this approach by observing and tasting plant parts at the beginning of each lesson. This lesson introduces the plant snack process with a buffet of all the edible plant parts children will study during the unit. Encourage them to be food explorers as they taste and describe each item. During the lesson they will predict which plant snacks will be eaten by the most people, record their own selections, and finally analyze class data. They will repeat this food preference study at the end of the unit and compare the two sets of data. The lesson ends with children drawing and writing their perceptions about plants in their journals.

What You Need

Plant Snack Items (at least 4 cut pieces of each item per child)
Choose a snack representing each of the six parts of a plant such as:
   ❋ carrots or jicama (roots)
   ❋ asparagus, kohlrabi, or broccoli stems (stems)
   ❋ celery, spinach, or red cabbage (leaves)
   ❋ broccoli crowns, cauliflower, or nasturtiums (flowers)
   ❋ red bell pepper, cucumber, cherry tomatoes, or raisins (fruits)
   ❋ almonds or fresh, shelled beans (seeds)

For Each Child
 ✳ journal
 ✳ pencil and crayons

For the Group
 ✳ uncut examples the plants used for snacks
 ✳ paper or index cards
 ✳ list of class norms for snack behavior
 ✳ How Do People Use Plants Chart
 ✳ What Plants Do I Eat Chart
 ✳ Food Preference Study Chart
 ✳ marking pens
 ✳ snack supplies: cutting board, knife, containers, spoons, plates, and napkins

Getting Ready

1. Before you start the unit, have students make their own botany journals (see Making a Botany Journal, below).

2. Develop class norms for snack behaviors a day or so before the unit begins. Help children

Making a Botany Journal

This journal is made entirely from materials that are plant stems. Children can decorate their cover by adding small leaves, flowers, and seeds.

Materials for Each Child
 ✳ 10 or more pieces of paper (full size or 5 1/2" x 8 1/2")
 ✳ 8 1/2"-long, straight stick
 ✳ medium or large rubber band
 ✳ 2 pieces of cardstock or heavy paper for covers (optional)

To Make the Journal
1. Place the paper between the coverstock and punch two holes about 1" from each edge.

2. From the back, thread the rubber band through one hole. Loop it around one end of the stick on the front.

3. Thread the other end of the rubber band up through the second hole and loop it around the other end of the stick.

4. Personalize the journal cover.

How Do People Use Plants?	
houses	fiber
clothes	perfume
food	cleaners
medicine	dyes
gardens	
decorating	
drinks	
tools	
to breathe!	

Food Preference Study		Totals
carrots	4, 4, 3, 2, 4, 3, 4, 2, 4, 4	34
asparagus	0, 1, 2, 2, 1, 0, 0, 1, 1, 1	9
celery	3, 4, 3, 2, 2, 3, 4, 3, 2, 3	29
cauliflower	1, 0, 1, 2, 0, 2, 2, 3, 1, 4	16
tomatoes	3, 4, 2, 3, 3, 4, 2, 3, 3, 2	29
almonds	2, 3, 4, 3, 4, 3, 3, 3, 4, 2	31

generate a list of respectful behaviors they would like to see in each other. Post their list as a reminder for future sessions.

3. Prepare the produce for the plant snacks so that the pieces are similar in size, and there are four pieces of each item per student and for yourself. Leave some of the produce uncut so children can see what the item originally looked like. Place each kind of snack in a separate container with the uncut example next to it. With a folded paper tent or index card, make a label for each snack with its name and the part of the plant it comes from (e.g., carrot, root). Just before the lesson, arrange the plant buffet with labels, plates, and napkins for easy access.

4. Make all three charts. To begin with, post the How Do People Use Plants Chart and the Food Preference Study Chart.

5. Have students wash their hands for the snack.

Prior Knowledge: How Do People Use Plants?

1. Present the How Do People Use Plants Chart and pose the question:

    ❀ *How do people use plants?* [wood for houses, medicine, beauty, shade, toys, fire, clothing, food]

    Encourage students to share their ideas while you record responses.

2. Circle the "food" suggestion and now post the What Plants Do I Eat Chart. Ask:

    ❀ *What plants do you eat?* Record all responses.

    (For answers such as "pizza," challenge the children to break down the food components to find plant items, such as tomatoes in the sauce.)

3. You will revisit these charts in Lesson 8 to allow children to enrich the lists, using a different color marker to show what they have learned.

Tastings and Journals: Food Preference Study

1. Tell children they will become scientists during the coming lessons as they underline investigate the amazing structures of plants. Botany is the study of plants, and scientists who study plants are called botanists. Early botanists were especially interested in food plants, so every session will begin with a plant snack to observe and eat.

> Underlined words are vocabulary words that can be found in the Glossary. You may want to write some of these on the board for students as you go.

2. Introduce each plant food featured in the snack buffet. Have children write the plant names in their journals as you list them on the Food Preference

Study Chart. (Leave enough room next to the plant name to add each child's data later in the lesson.) Ask children to underline in their journal the food they predict will be eaten by the most people.

3. Announce that you have prepared enough for everyone to have as many as four pieces of each type of food. Caution students to take only what they plan to eat, but encourage them to try at least one piece of an item they have never tasted. Have them form a line and make a snack plate for themselves.

4. Back at their desks, have students keep a tally as they snack by making a mark next to the plant name for each piece that they eat. (Review tallying for students not familiar with this counting method.)

5. Direct students to write down the total number of each item they ate once they are done snacking. As they finish they will come to the board with their journals and write their totals next to the plant foods on the Food Preference Study Chart. Students should record a zero if no pieces of an item were eaten.

6. While students wait for their peers to finish, encourage them to document plant observations in their journals through writing or drawing.

Which Plants Were Eaten Most and Least?

1. Invite children to suggest ways to determine which foods were eaten most and least. Have them consider the class totals data on the board. Depending on the grade level of your students, there are a number of approaches you can take — you want them to practice their math reasoning skills within the time constraints of the session.

2. Encourage children to discuss their ideas with each other, just as scientists discuss findings with each other. Give them about five minutes to consider the evidence and to write their conclusions in their journals, then have children report their results. They may decide to add up the items eaten for each food and compare the totals. Or they might want to find the average amount of pieces eaten for each food. What if an item was tried by everyone, but not a lot of pieces were eaten? Or tried only by a few who ate a lot of pieces? Remind students to consider how many zero entries a food item has in determining which was eaten by the most people.

3. Record the results on the Food Preference Study Chart. Ask how the children's predictions about the food eaten by the most people compared with the results.

Reflecting on the Lesson

1. Refer back to the charts and explain that people from cultures all over the world have been using plants for thousands of years. We know a lot about plants today because many people before us have recorded and shared what they found.

2. Over the centuries, people have <u>bred</u> plants from the wild to exhibit the vast array of traits we now see in cultivated edible plants (like the plump sweetness of a carrot root or the bright purple color of a cabbage). As the class looks at edible plants in the coming lessons, tell students to keep in mind that each plant part (roots, for example) can come in many different shapes and sizes. Give them a few minutes to write their comparisons of the snack items (appearance, taste, texture).

3. Point out that there are still many mysteries about plants, and there is a need for plant scientists. Invite children to become botanists with you as they gather evidence, compare results, and record findings in their journals.

4. To close the lesson, ask children to draw a <u>diagram</u> of a plant in their journal.

5. The charts and journal entries provide information about what the children know already, and will assist you in assessing growth in their knowledge. Date the charts and save them for use in future sessions, when you can document new things that students have learned using different colored markers. Save the Food Preference Study Chart for Chapter 8.

More Questions to Investigate

❀ *What plants do my relatives eat?* Have children find out and share some plant ingredients that are often used in their family's kitchen, from vegetables to spices. Ask, *Does your family eat any traditional foods?*

❀ *What foods do you like now that you didn't eat when you were younger?* Focus on fruits, vegetables, seeds, and nuts. Help students notice that some things can be an acquired taste.

❀ *What are some ways to encourage people to taste new plant foods?*

❀ *What are some plant-oriented careers?* Have students research careers that involve people and plants. Examples include landscape design, farming, genetic research, integrated pest management, arboriculture, herbal medicine.

Roots

ROOT FUNCTIONS:
absorb water and nutrients;
anchor the plant; store food

After tasting and comparing root snacks, children observe, dissect, and draw a radish plant, describing external features (such as root hairs) and internal structures. The group shares ideas and evidence about the ways roots help the plant absorb water and nutrients, and anchor it in the soil. Next, students compare and contrast fibrous roots with the radish taproot, noting the food-storing adaptation. Finally, they apply what they have learned as they examine new examples of roots that people eat.

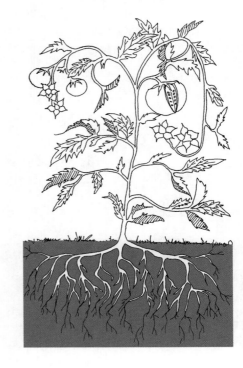

What You Need

Plant Snack Items (at least 4 cut pieces of each item per child)
* ❋ carrot and/or jicama pieces
* ❋ radish slices

Dissection Materials for Student Pairs
* ❋ 2 radishes with leaves and obvious root hairs
* ❋ paper plate or cutting board
* ❋ dissection knives
* ❋ magnifier
* ❋ journals
* ❋ pencils and crayons
* ❋ 30-centimeter ruler
* ❋ Root Nutrition Labels (carrot and jicama, p. 70)

For the Group
* ❋ uncut example of each plant snack item
* ❋ Structures of a Tomato Plant diagram (p. 65)
* ❋ 11"x 2" paper sentence strips and tape
* ❋ classroom board or chart paper
* ❋ marking pens
* ❋ 1-2 examples of fibrous roots with leaves attached (wild or lawn grass, wheat grass, or lettuce)
* ❋ snack supplies: cutting board, knife, containers, spoons, plates, and napkins
* ❋ additional roots: choose taproots with root hairs and leaves attached if possible (see Plant Products Kit, p. 12, and Produce Shopping List by Lesson, p. 13)

Getting Ready

1. Before starting this lesson, familiarize students with nutrition labels and the information they contain (see How to Read a Nutrition Facts Label, p. 69).

2. Purchase produce that has not been treated with pesticides. Farmers' markets usually have a great selection of organic produce that is less processed than grocery store produce (root crops, for instance, will have more root hairs). Select root examples for the science dissection that have root hairs and leaf tops attached. Wash the produce that students will taste. Bags of processed baby carrots are fine to use for snacks, but not for dissection.

3. Dig up a grass plant or small lettuce and shake most, but not all, of the soil from the roots. Store it in a clear plastic bag so that children can observe the roots clinging to soil.

4. Cut the jicama vertically and save a portion to display the outside covering and root hairs. Peel and dice the rest for students to taste during their snack time. Slice several radishes for students to taste. Make a name card for each kind of root that will be displayed during the lesson.

5. Make copies of the Root Nutrition Labels, and cut the paper sentence strips.

6. Just before the session, organize the dissecting materials, the produce, and the plant snacks that students will taste.

1. Write Root: Radish and the date.
2. Use a magnifier to examine the radish.
3. Draw the outside of the radish plant. Add a dotted line where you will make a cut.
4. Cut the radish and examine the inside.
5. Draw the inside of the radish. Measure, record, and label the diameter.
6. Color the drawing by rubbing the plant parts on the paper.

7. Copy the Structures of a Tomato Plant diagram large enough for children to see it clearly and color the drawing accurately. Sketch a radish plant on the board or a piece of paper, being as detailed as possible, including tiny root hairs at the "tail" of the radish. This will encourage your students to make detailed drawings in their journals. Write the dissection steps shown in the illustration (left) on the board or a piece of chart paper.

Tastings and Journals

1. Have children take out their journals and get ready for the snack.

2. Referring to the colored-in Structures of a Tomato Plant diagram, ask students:
   - ❀ *What kind of a plant does this look like? How do you know?* [the fruit looks like a tomato]
   - ❀ *What other way might you be able to tell what kind of a plant this is if it did not have fruits yet?* [shape of leaves; color of flower]

3. Show that there are six main parts of a plant, pointing to them on the diagram as you go: roots, stems, leaves, flowers, fruits, and seeds. Explain that students will investigate each major plant part. Today they will start with the roots.

4. Display a whole carrot with its leafy top and a jicama root, and announce that students will taste and observe the part of these plants that is hidden underground. Write on the board and have students title their journal page "<u>Root</u>" and record the date.

5. Have students get their root snacks. Tell the children to taste and observe the plant part using all of their senses.

6. Distribute the Root Nutrition Labels and ask:

   ❀ *What are some important nutrients that our body gets from plant snacks?* [<u>vitamins</u>, <u>minerals</u>, fiber, carbohydrates, water, protein, fats, and oils]

   ❀ *Looking at the nutrition labels, which nutrients are our snacks high in?*

7. Encourage students to share and write as many adjectives as they can to describe the smell, taste, appearance, and texture of the snacks. During the discussion, record their adjectives on paper strips that you post on a word wall for children to use later in the unit.

Dissecting Roots to Explore Structure

1. Hold up a radish plant and ask who recognizes it. Have children add the word "Radish" to their journal entry and tell them that they will use all of their senses to examine both the outside and inside of the radish root. Display your sketch of the plant and demonstrate how to use the natural pigments in the radish to color the drawing. (Rub the radish on the paper for red; rub the leaves for green.)

2. Explain that pairs of children will <u>dissect</u> radishes. Dissection is a method scientists use to carefully cut open and look at the structures inside of something. Note that because these plants are being used scientifically, there will be no eating of plants during the dissection. Children may taste washed plant parts again at the end of the lesson.

3. On your sketch, draw dotted lines that <u>bisect</u> the radish root horizontally and vertically. Explain that one student per pair will make either a <u>vertical</u> or <u>horizontal</u> cut to their radish. Students should draw one of these lines on their journal sketch to show which way they will make their cut.

4. If students will be making their own cuts, provide safety directions as you demonstrate how to use a knife to make a horizontal cut. (See Using Dissecting Tools, p. 25.)

5. Review the dissection steps listed on the board. Distribute the radishes and equipment and have the children begin their observations. Encourage them to make detailed measurements and drawings and record their observations.

6. As you circulate among the students, draw the children's attention to the tiny root hairs coming off the bottom of the radish. Ask, *How long are the root hairs?* [1 to 3 millimeters] Remind students to use their magnifier to see small details, patterns, and irregularities and to add these to their drawings.

Root Function Ideas Based on Observations

1. Allow a few minutes for each pair to share observations with another pair and to write at least two <u>characteristics</u> in their journals. Depending on the children's literacy level, have them include complete sentences describing the radish and dissection procedure.

2. Make two columns on the board for observations titled "Outside" and "Inside." Ask each pair in turn to share an observation. List all observations on the board, continuing the reporting as long as pairs still have new characteristics to share.

3. Guide students in sharing their knowledge and ideas about the functions of roots based on what they have observed. Pose questions such as:

   ❀ *Why do you think the radish was moist inside?* [the root pulls in water from the soil]

   ❀ *How did water get inside the radish root?* [absorbed by root hairs at the bottom]

4. Draw attention to the observation of little threads or "hairs" coming out of the bottom of the radish root.

   ❀ *How do hairs coming off the root help the radish plant?* [extend its reach for water; <u>anchor</u> the plant in the ground]

5. Explain that <u>root hairs</u> are the tiny structures that go between individual pieces of soil. Each of these root hairs is surrounded by many more <u>microscopic</u> root hairs that <u>absorb</u> <u>water</u> and <u>nutrients</u>. Having root hairs is a way we can decide if an underground plant part is actually a root. (This characteristic will be a helpful distinction for the Stem lesson.)

6. From the list of "inside" radish observations, note the dotted pattern (like tops of straws) from the horizontal cut and the tube-like structures from the vertical cut.

   ❀ *How might water get from the roots to the rest of the plant?* [goes up tubes]

Two Different Types of Roots

1. Display the grass plant and carrot plant side by side, and ask students:

   ❀ *How are these roots different?* [grass roots are thin with many strands; the carrot root is singular and fat]

2. Explain that botanists use the terms <u>fibrous root</u> to describe the stringy roots of the grass

plant, and <u>taproot</u> to describe the fat, solid root of the carrot plant. In comparing the roots, ask:

❀ *Which kind of root might be specially <u>adapted</u> to store food? What evidence supports your idea?* [taproot; it is large, moist, colored, sweet]

❀ *Which would you rather eat? Which would hold more energy and be more nutritious?*

❀ *Which kind of root is the radish?* [taproot]

Reflecting on the Investigation

1. Solicit from the group the main functions of roots for the plant, and write these on the Structures of a Tomato Plant diagram on the line for roots. [absorb water and nutrients; anchor the plant; store food]

2. Present the additional examples of edible roots and rotate them through teams of students to observe and compare to the radish. If you have a sweet potato among your examples,

Using Dissecting Tools

We encourage you to teach children safe procedures for using small paring knives to dissect produce. If the ages and numbers of your students prevent their direct use of science tools, you and classroom aides may rotate among the pairs with a dissecting knife to assist with the cuts. Second grade teachers have reported success using the following approach with their children.

1. We will use knives as scientific tools to dissect the plant parts. *How many of you have used knives at home?*

2. Let's make a list of safety steps we will follow:
   ✳ Hold the point away from yourself and others.
   ✳ Only make cuts while using a cutting board or stable surface.
   ✳ Keep your fingers away from the area to be cut.
   ✳ Make a steady cut straight down and not at a slant or toward you.
   ✳ Hold the handle and steady the knife with your index finger along the blunt, top edge of the knife.
   ✳ Set the knife aside in a safe place.

3. You and your partner will each make one cut today, so it is very important to plan your cut carefully.

explain that this kind of root is called a root <u>tuber</u>. The sweet potato plant stores food in the form of starch in these fleshy roots.

3. Circulate among the teams and provide prompts as needed:

❀ *How is this root the same as or different from the radish?*

❀ *What do botanists call this kind of a root?* [taproot or fibrous root]

❀ *What is something interesting you have learned about roots?*

❀ *What do you still wonder about roots?*

Going Further

Root Math: Measuring

❀ Volume: How much space do root crops like carrots and rutabagas take up in the ground? Use a container big enough for your food items, a substance like lentils or barley to fill the container, and a measuring scoop. First, count how many scoops of your filler it takes to fill the empty container, and then, how many scoops with a root inside the container. *Why did it take fewer scoops? How many "scoops" does the root occupy?* Subtract the first count from the second count and you have your root's volume in "scoops." Make volume predictions and measurements for roots with various shapes.

❀ Length and Weight: Have students harvest root vegetables from the garden, and use string and rulers to find the length and circumference of each item picked. Then use balance scales to find their weights. Students can compare their measurements and discuss how the practice of measuring and weighing root crops is helpful to farmers.

Root Nutrition: How to Read a Nutrition Facts Label

❀ Use the Carrot and Jicama Nutrition Labels as examples for learning how to read the information on a nutrition facts label. How to Read a Nutrition Facts Label (p. 69) offers a guide to this information. Children can apply their knowledge to packaged foods.

Root Cooking and Social Science: Botany In Your Soup

❀ Tell students that soup was invented about 5,000 years ago and that the science of making soup profoundly improved the survival of the people who invented it. Heating water to its boiling point (212°F) killed waterborne parasites, made grains and roots more easily digestible, and provided warmth. Early cultures learned to make soup in clay pots, finely woven baskets, and skin bags to which were added small rocks heated in a fire.

As a class project, use the edible roots from this lesson to make a soup. Rinse any dissected plant parts, and add them to a pot of water that has been seasoned with salt and herbs. Simmer the ingredients for about an hour to kill all microorganisms and allow the flavors of the roots to blend into a delicious soup. Some good candidates for root soup include carrots, sweet potatoes, celeriac, and parsnips.

Root Language Arts: Reading Stories

❧ Many wonderful children's stories feature root crops. Some examples are *Tops and Bottoms*, *The Gigantic Turnip*, *Stone Soup,* and *The Tale of Peter Rabbit.* Choose a few to read aloud or add to your library in conjunction with this lesson.

Root Science: Hydroponics

❧ Show students a variety of roots and ask what they think might happen if roots are suspended in water. Following the directions, set up the Sweet Potato Root Hydroponics experiment (below).

Give students time to draw the sweet potato root, and talk and write about their ideas. Guide them to develop a hypothesis for the experiment, as well as a schedule for observing and documenting any changes in the root over a period of weeks.

Do not tell students that in about a week, a stem will begin to grow out of the top, and root hairs will grow from the lower end.

Sweet Potato Root Hydroponics

A sweet potato plant stores food in thick, starchy roots called root tubers. Use one of these roots for the following experiment.

What You Need
 * sweet potato root
 * clear glass or jar
 * 3 toothpicks
 * water

Grow a Plant in Water

1. Fill a glass about 1/2 full with water.

2. Stick toothpicks into the root like spokes of a wheel so they encircle the lower portion of the sweet potato.

3. Position the sweet potato in the glass so the toothpicks rest on the rim and the bottom 1/3 of the root is immersed in water; the stem end (it usually looks cut) should be above the water.

4. Place the glass in a bright area, but not in direct sunlight.

5. Add water as needed so the bottom of the sweet potato remains covered.

6. Have students keep a record of the changes they observe.

Stems

STEM FUNCTIONS: transport water and nutrients; hold up plant parts; store food

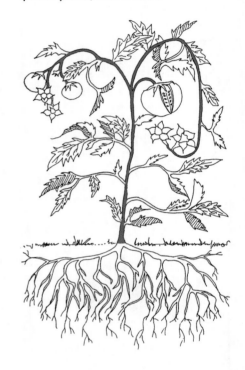

Children observe the tube-like structures in the stem that transport water and nutrients from the roots to other parts of the plant. They discuss evidence that the stem supports the plant and connects the roots with the rest of the plant. In an experiment with a daisy and food coloring, children generate hypotheses, observations, and explanations about water transportation through the stem. During a wrap up, they compare several edible stems and products made from stems such as wood and rubber that are important for housing and transportation.

What You Need

Plant Snack Items (at least 4 cut pieces of each item per child)
  ❋ asparagus, kohlrabi, and/or broccoli stems

Dissection Materials for Student Pairs
  ❋ asparagus stalk — prepared with blue dye
  ❋ paper plate or cutting board
  ❋ dissection knives
  ❋ magnifier
  ❋ journals
  ❋ pencils and crayons
  ❋ 30-centimeter ruler
  ❋ Stem Nutrition Labels (asparagus and kohlrabi, p. 71)

For the Group
  ❋ uncut example of each snack item
  ❋ undyed asparagus spear
  ❋ white Gerber daisy
  ❋ mint or basil stem showing leaf nodes
  ❋ 4-6 aging green potatoes with eyes
  ❋ nopales cactus pad (or picture of one)
  ❋ blue and red food coloring
  ❋ 2 small clear glasses or seasoning jars
  ❋ pencil
  ❋ Structures of a Tomato Plant diagram (from Lesson 2)
  ❋ How Do People Use Plants Chart (from Lesson 1)
  ❋ 11"x 2" paper sentence strips and tape
  ❋ classroom board or chart paper

✳ marking pens

✳ snack supplies: cutting board, knife, containers, spoons, plates, and napkins

✳ additional stems: have on hand a few other examples listed in the Plant Products Kit, p. 12, and Produce Shopping List by Lesson, p. 13.

Getting Ready

1. If necessary, several weeks before you begin the activity, expose potatoes to light until they start to develop growths from some of the nodes, commonly called "eyes."

2. Wash and prepare the produce for the snack. You may want to peel the tough outer skins of kohlrabi or broccoli stems before slicing them into rounds. Quarter the asparagus spears lengthwise into thin sticks. Keep some produce uncut so children can see what the plants look like.

3. Cut off the bottom inch of the asparagus spears the class will use for dissection. Place the spears, cut end down, in about a cup of water to which you have added enough blue food dye (about 10 drops) to turn it deep blue. (If asparagus is unavailable use broccoli crowns that have florets attached to long stems.) Place the container of spears in a warm, sunny location to stimulate the flow of water up the stems.

> The stems require several hours in the food coloring *before* dissection to allow the stems to thoroughly absorb the dye. You can set this up the day before and leave it overnight. The stems must have their tops intact for the blue dye to be drawn upward by the transpiration of water through the top.

4. For the daisy demonstration, purchase a white Gerber daisy with a thick, sturdy stem, and keep it in water until the demonstration. (If a Gerber daisy is not available, choose another white, multi-petaled flower with a thick stem, such as a lily.) To set up the demonstration tape 2 small, clear glasses (or seasoning bottles) together. Tape a pencil vertically to the edge where the containers join to provide support for the flower. Fill the glasses about half full with water and add blue food coloring to one and red to the other until the water in each is deeply colored.

5. Just before the session, organize the dissecting materials, produce, and plants that students will taste.

1. Write Stem: Asparagus and the date.

2. Observe and draw the stem.

3. Draw a dotted horizontal line 1" inch from the bottom of the stem where you will make the first cut. Draw a dotted vertical line from top to bottom of the stem where you will make the second cut.

4. Make the horizontal cut, then the vertical cut.

5. Use a magnifier to examine the inside of the stem.

6. Draw the inside of the stem.

6. Post the Structures of a Tomato Plant diagram, and have on hand the How Do People Use Plants Chart that you created in Lesson 1.

7. Draw an asparagus stem on the board and list the steps for the dissection as shown in the illustration (left).

Tastings and Journals

1. Have children take out their journals and get ready for the tastings. Draw their attention to the diagram of the tomato plant. Ask what they remember about roots and review root functions.

2. Hold up an asparagus and ask what part of the plant they think it represents. Confirm an identification of *stem*, and have them title their journal page "<u>Stem</u>" along with the word "Asparagus" and the date. As you introduce the foods for tasting, show the uncut examples.

3. Review the procedures for observing, tasting, and recording findings in journals. Encourage children to experience the stem snacks using all of their senses and to explore each snack item's nutrients using the Stem Nutrition Labels. Discuss stem snack characteristics and add new descriptive adjectives to the word wall.

Dissecting Stems to Explore Structure

1. Display the asparagus still soaking in blue water. Explain that students will dissect stems that that have been soaking for a while in blue food coloring to provide clues about the movement of water in a plant. Review the dissection procedures on the board and the safety measures botanists use to dissect plants.

2. Using an undyed asparagus spear, demonstrate how to make horizontal and vertical cuts. Review this vocabulary and add these cuts as dotted lines on your drawing. Tell students that this asparagus has not been soaking in blue water and show them what it looks like inside.

3. Explain that each partner will make one cut. One partner first makes a horizontal cut near the bottom of the stem (above, right), creating a short "log." The other partner then cuts the long segment lengthwise in half (below). It is important to make this cut as straight as possible in the center of the stem, from top to bottom.

4. Distribute the dyed stems and equipment and ask the students to begin observing and documenting. Remind them to use the magnifiers to see small details and <u>patterns</u>.

5. As you circulate among the children, ask questions to spark their thinking about what they see.

   ❋ *What might the triangle shapes on the outside of the stem be?* [leaves]

   ❋ *What is at the top of the stem?* [leaf and flower buds]

6. Draw children's attention to the different patterns of blue dye.

❂ *What parts of the stem are dyed blue?*

❂ *What pattern did the horizontal cut reveal?* [ring of tiny blue dots]

❂ *What did the vertical cut reveal?* [thin blue lines] *How far do the lines go?* [to the top of the stem]

❂ *What does the vertically cut stem look like when you view it from the bottom, half-circle end?* [dotted]

❂ *What happened while the asparagus was sitting in the water?* [water was transported up the stem]

7. As pairs complete their dissections, have them record their findings in their journals, including the length of the longest blue line. Then have them share their observations with another pair.

Stem Function Ideas Based on Observations

1. Encourage children to share their stem observations and write them on the board. Ask:

❂ *What caused the blue color in the stem?* [the water that had been dyed blue]

❂ *Where did you see blue on the stem?*

❂ *In what manner did it travel from the cup of water through the inside of the stem?* [in straight lines or tubes]

2. The vertical cut reveals long tubes extending from the bottom to the top of the stem. These tubes, called <u>xylem</u>, conduct the water from the roots to the rest of the plant.

3. What about the dots? Have students think about a straw in a glass of water. Ask, *What does the straw look like from the top?* [a circle] The blue dots from the horizontal cut are like looking down at the tops of the tubes.

4. Guide students in sharing their knowledge and ideas about the functions of stems that relate to things they have observed.

❂ *What do you think stems do for plants?* [transport water; hold up other plant parts such as leaves]

❂ *What evidence have you observed to support your ideas?* [stems have tubes that turned blue when put in colored water; asparagus is stiff with little leaves on the sides; leaves also became tinged with blue]

❂ *How might stems help a plant growing in a shady environment?* [help leaves reach sunlight; prevent animals from stepping on plant]

Stem Nodes and Adaptations

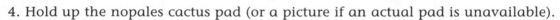

1. Display the mint or basil stem example that shows leaves coming out of <u>nodes</u> on the stem. Explain that botanists have determined that all stems have nodes where buds, leaves, and flowers form.

2. Distribute the green potatoes and encourage students to observe the skin and sprouting eyes, or nodes, of the potato. Have them consider what they know about roots [have root hairs] and what they have learned about stems. Ask,

   ❀ *What evidence do you find on the potato that may make it a stem part of the plant and not a root?* [no root hairs; green color; nodes]

3. Explain that although potatoes grow underground, botanists classify them as a stem part and not a root. The potato plant has fibrous roots. Instead of storing food in its roots, it stores food in underground offshoots of the stem called tubers. Like sweet potatoes, potatoes store food in the form of starch, but the potato and the sweet potato are two different parts of a plant. If left in sunlight, potato skins will turn green (like the stem) and a stem and leaves will grow from the nodes. New roots with root hairs will grow from the new stem, not from the potato itself. A potato cannot be a root because roots do not have nodes and do not have green pigment.

4. Hold up the nopales cactus pad (or a picture if an actual pad is unavailable).

   ❀ *What part of the plant do you think the cactus pad is? Why?*

   Point out that the nodes on the pad make it a stem. The spines coming from the nodes are its modified leaves. The wide stem of the cactus has special tissue that can store water.

   ❀ *How might these <u>adaptations</u> help a desert plant?* [can survive limited rainfall with stored water; has less sun exposure and water loss by not having broad, flat leaves; spines deter animals that would eat it]

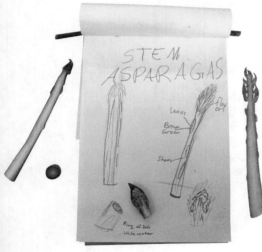

Reflecting on the Investigation

1. Solicit from the group the main functions of stems and add these to your Structures of a Tomato Plant diagram. [transport water and nutrients; join and hold up other parts of the plant]

2. Share with the group the additional examples of stem items you have selected. Distribute them to teams of students to observe, smell, and feel.

   ❀ Why do we eat very few stems? [they tend to be tough to hold up the plant, therefore not very good to eat]

❀ *What are some ways that people use stems besides for food?* [to make paper, harvest tree sap to make rubber for tires and equipment, building materials]

3. Revisit your How Do People Use Plants Chart and identify any uses listed that come from stems. Add new examples using a different colored marker.

4. Ask if anyone knows what the tallest living <u>organism</u> is. It is the coast redwood tree, *Sequoia sempervirens,* and it gets its height from its incredible stem.

Applying Stem Knowledge: A Daisy Stem Experiment

1. Announce that students will work together as scientists on an experiment that will provide more evidence for how water moves up the stems of plants.

2. Show students the glass containers of red- and blue-dyed water and the white daisy.

3. First trim the stem so the flower head will stand about 4 inches above the glass containers. (The shorter the stem, the faster the dyed water will arrive at the flower.) Starting at the trimmed end of the stem, carefully bisect the lower 4 to 5 inches of stem with a vertical cut. Make the cut as straight as possible. Immerse one part of the bisected stem in the blue dye and the other part in the red. Be careful not to break the stem as you spread the halves apart.

4. Use tape to stabilize the flower against the pencil, and set the experiment in a warm sunny location that students can view easily. Ask the class:

   ❀ *What will happen if we put a cut daisy stem in two different colors of water?*

5. Tell students that as scientists they will propose several <u>hypotheses</u>. (If this is a new term for them, explain that it is an idea or prediction that can guide an investigation.) Write the first part of a hypothesis on the board:

   When a daisy stem that's been cut vertically has half its stem in red dye and half in blue dye:

6. Record student response on the board. Examples may include:

   – *The petals will turn purple.*

   – *The petals on the blue side will turn blue and the other half will turn red.*

   – *Petal color will alternate blue, red, blue, red.*

   – *The dye will stop where the cut in the stem ends.*

7. While giving the experiment time to work, share the additional stem examples. Have a volunteer check the daisy every 10 minutes, or after a break.

True Statements about the Daisy Experiment

1. Revisit the daisy experiment and have partners discuss their observations. Tell the students you will then list their observations on paper strips in the form of sentences that make <u>true statements</u> and post them on the board under the heading "Evidence." Ask:

   ❀ *How did the daisy change?*

2. Ask volunteers to report their observations as evidence. A child might say, *"The daisy turned half blue and half pink."* Post the sentence, and encourage others to further define this observation. Another child might suggest, *"The petals on the side with blue water turned blue and the petals on the side with red water turned pink."*

3. If some students disagree with the wording of a statement, point out that scientists frequently work together to make their reports more accurate. Have them help the first student to rephrase the statement so that it is supported by the observations.

4. Revisit the term "hypothesis," and ask if the true statements provide support for any of the ideas and predictions on the list. Have students identify one or more hypotheses that are supported by the true statements.

5. Create a new heading on the board titled "<u>Explanations</u>," and encourage students to list their ideas on sentence strips:

   – *The dye in the water travels up the stem to the petal.*

   – *The tubes continue from the stem to the petal.*

   – *Tubes on one side of the stem connect to petals on the same side.*

6. Point out that investigations usually lead to more questions. Ask if students can suggest some new questions related to their stem studies. Write their questions on sentence strips and save or post them under a "Questions" heading.

Going Further

Stem Math: Rate of Travel

❀ *How does heat affect the rate at which water travels up a stem?* Have students put fresh asparagus spears in several cups with equal amounts of blue-dyed water. Place the cups in different locations with varying temperatures, such as in a refrigerator or on a sunny or shady windowsill. Leave the containers for 1 hour. (The time needed for the dye to travel up the stems will vary based on other conditions as well, such as light and humidity.) Cut the spears in half vertically from top to bottom and measure the line of blue water with a centimeter ruler. Ask, *How many centimeters per hour did the water travel? In what ways did you ensure your experiment was a fair test?*

Stem Nutrition and Cooking: Asparagus and Kohlrabi

❀ Children may report that they don't like a vegetable, but that's often due to how it has been prepared for them. Boiling a vegetable usually destroys both its taste and its nutrients. Try steaming asparagus, kohlrabi, or broccoli stems until they're just tender and have students try them. As they examine the Stem Nutrition Labels, point out that vitamin C can easily break down in the cooking process.

Stem Science and Social Science: Maple Syrup

❀ Remind students that sometimes plants store food. Ask, *Where does this food come from?* Tell students that stems have a second type of tube-like structure that transports the sugars and food made in the leaves to other parts of the plant, including down to the roots. (You will talk more about this food-making process in the Leaf lesson.) These tubes are the long thin phloem cells, which are located just inside the outer covering of the stem. For instance, Native Americans harvested the sweet sap of maple trees by making cuts in the bark and collecting the sap as it flowed from the cuts. Today, farmers still tap maple trees and boil the sap to make maple syrup.

Stem Language Arts: Similes

❀ Have students create similes by using adjectives that describe stems. For example, "as tough as nails," "as straight as an arrow," "as tall as…," or "as strong as…."

Leaves

LEAF FUNCTION: make food (photosynthesis)

Children examine the patterns of veins on several leaves, and trace blue food coloring along the water transport tubes. They learn that leaves make food for the plant, and that green chlorophyll captures the sun's energy and transforms water and carbon dioxide gas into sugar. This process, known as photosynthesis, takes place primarily in the leaf. Students draw a leaf and color it green by rubbing the chlorophyll pigment from a green leaf onto their paper. They compare and discuss a variety of edible leaves.

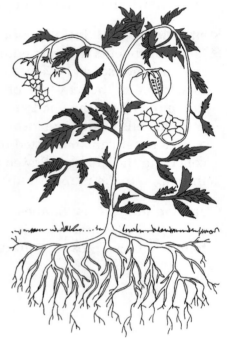

What you need

Plant Snack Items (at least 4 cut pieces of each item per child)
- ✻ celery sticks
- ✻ red cabbage strips

Dissection Materials for Student Pairs
- ✻ 2 mint leaves
- ✻ leafy celery stalks prepared with blue dye
- ✻ magnifier
- ✻ paper plate or cutting board
- ✻ dissection knives
- ✻ journals
- ✻ pencils and crayons
- ✻ Leaf Nutrition Labels (romaine and iceberg lettuce, p. 72)

For the Group
- ✻ uncut example of each snack item
- ✻ demonstration mint and celery leaves
- ✻ paper
- ✻ Structures of a Tomato Plant diagram (from Lesson 2)
- ✻ Photosynthesis diagram (p. 66)
- ✻ 11"x 2" paper sentence strips and tape
- ✻ classroom board or chart paper
- ✻ marking pens
- ✻ snack supplies: cutting board, knife, containers, spoons, plates, and napkins
- ✻ additional leaves: choose a selection that includes herbs, onions, and greens (see Plant Products Kit, p. 12, and Produce Shopping List by Lesson, p. 13)

Getting Ready

1. Wash and prepare the celery and cabbage for the snack and the mint leaves for the dissection. Cut a celery bunch with leafy tops in half lengthwise, so the stalks remain attached to the core base. Set one half aside. Similarly, reserve a wedge of the cabbage head that shows the leaves attached to its white core.

> The celery must be put into the food coloring at least an hour before class to allow the dye time to travel up the full length of the leaf.

2. To demonstrate water flow in leaf veins, cut off the bottom half-inch of stalks (including the core) from the other piece of celery. Put the cut ends in a container of water dyed with 4 to 5 drops of blue food coloring. Place in a warm, sunny location to stimulate the flow of water up the leaves.

3. Just before the lesson, rinse the dyed celery, and organize the dissecting materials, produce, and plants that students will taste.

4. Draw a celery leaf on the board, and list the steps for the dissection as shown in the illustration (right).

> 1. Write Leaf: Celery, Mint, and the date.
> 2. Make a vein "rubbing" of the mint.
> 3. Observe and draw the celery. Add dotted lines to your drawing where you will make cuts.
> 4. Make the horizontal and vertical cuts and observe the celery with a magnifier.
> 5. Draw the cross sections.
> 6. Rub green pigment from the celery or mint leaf onto the celery drawing.

Tastings and Journals

1. Have children take out their journals and prepare for the tastings. Review what they remember about roots and stems and their functions. Hold up the uncut celery and the cabbage wedge and ask:

   ❀ *What part of the plant do you think these represent?* [leaves]

2. Accept their suggestions and propose that the group discuss evidence after the plant dissections. Encourage children to share ideas with a partner while they are eating.

3. If necessary, review with students the procedures for observing, tasting, and recording their findings in their journals.

Dissecting Leaves to Explore Structures

1. Tell students they will take a closer look at a mint leaf by creating a texture rubbing that will reveal its veins. Next they will dissect and draw celery that has been soaked in blue food coloring to provide clues about the movement of water in the plant. Tell them to write "leaf: celery, mint" in their journals along with the date. Review the procedures and safety measures that botanists use to dissect plants.

2. First, demonstrate how to make a "leaf rubbing" by placing a mint leaf — with the bumpy side up — under a piece of paper. Using the side of a pencil or crayon, gently rub back and forth over the area of the leaf until clear edges and veins emerge. Suggest that before

children make their rubbing they hold the leaf up to the light to illuminate the leaf's patterns and structures.

3. Next, demonstrate how to make a horizontal cut at the base of the stick of celery and a vertical cut along its entire length. Indicate these as dashed lines on your celery drawing. Point out that partners will take turns cutting the stalk.

4. Distribute the leaves and begin the documenting and dissecting. As you circulate among pairs of students, draw their attention to the tube-like structures and top leaflets of the celery stalks that have been dyed blue. Direct them to compare the horizontal and vertical cuts. The horizontal cut reveals tiny circles encircling the base of the stalk; the vertical cut reveals long tubes extending up the stalk into the leaflets. Ask,

❀ *Why are these tubes blue?* [transported the blue water]

❀ *Where else in a plant have you observed colored tubes?* [root, stem, flower petals]

❀ *How do you think these tubes are related to the other tubes?* [they are all part of the water transport system that goes from the roots throughout the plant]

5. Remind children to color their drawings by rubbing the green pigment from the celery or mint onto their drawings.

6. Ask students to identify two to three characteristics that are common to both plants. Allow a few minutes for each pair of students to write in their journals and share observations with another pair.

Leaf Parts

1. As a group, have each pair in turn report one common trait (from Step 6) as you list the observations on the board. Continue until pairs can no longer report a similarity that hasn't already been listed. Ask,

❀ *How are the mint and celery similar?* [tubes/veins, green color, moisture/water, jagged edges, smelly]

2. Conduct a survey and tally how many pairs saw each similarity. Total how many found tubes or veins and ask,

❀ *How are celery stalks like stems?* [stiff; have tubes that transport water]

❀ *What evidence did you find that the celery stalks are leaves?* [have leaflets at the top; veins]

3. Show the students the reserved half bunch of celery. Tell them this is a single celery plant that's been cut in half, and it has just one stem. Walk around the room to give students a closer look and ask them to consider what the stem might be.

4. After soliciting their ideas, tell students that the celery plant stem is only a thin disk of tissue at the base of the stalks, which is easy to overlook. The part of celery we eat is actually a

leaf. The tough stalk is actually a modified <u>petiole</u> — the part of the leaf that connects the <u>blade</u> to the stem. Over time, farmers have bred the plant to have these enlarged, fleshy leaf petioles. A celery stalk is one leaf with a top blade that divides into leaflets.

Rather than growing upward, the celery stem is a thin disc that grows outward, with new leaves developing at the center and mature leaves on the outside, creating the plant's overlapping, bunched shape.

5. Have students find the petiole on their mint leaf (the stick-like part where it was attached to the stem) and the rounded blade. Have students label their mint rubbing and celery drawing with the two parts of a leaf: petiole and blade.

6. Show students the reserved red cabbage wedge and identify its short white core as the stem, with red leaves attached.

Leaves as the Food Factory

1. Ask students:

   ❀ *What do plants need to live?* [sun, water, air]

   Tell students that what is amazing about plants is that they can use these elements to make their own food. This "food factory" typically resides in the leaves.

2. Ask if anyone knows the name of the green substance in the leaves that they used to color their drawings. Write the term <u>chlorophyll</u> on the board. Explain that it is this incredible chemical that gives plants the ability to capture the energy of sunlight and use the energy to make sugar and other substances that are food for the plant. Explain that the leaf requires water, absorbed by the roots, and <u>carbon dioxide</u> gas from the air to carry out this process, known as <u>photosynthesis</u>. Use the Photosynthesis diagram to help describe the process.

Photosynthesis is a very complex process that is difficult even for adults to understand. These direct observations and investigations will help students form a basic vocabulary and experiences as a foundation for understanding plant physiology taught in later grades.

3. The food substances made in the leaves then travel back through the rest of the plant through tube-like structures called <u>phloem</u>, sustaining the plant and allowing it to grow. This food is also sometimes stored in various parts of the plant.

4. Through the process of photosynthesis the plant also produces a gas that it releases into the air. Ask if students know the name of this gas; confirm that it is <u>oxygen</u>, the gas we — and all animals — need to breathe.

Leaf Function Ideas Based on Observations

1. Guide students in sharing their knowledge and ideas about the functions of leaves and the things they have observed. Ask,

   ❀ *What do you think leaves do for a plant?* [transport water; absorb sunlight; make food for the plant]

❀ *What evidence have you observed to support your ideas?* [veins in leaves; tubes that turn blue when put in colored water; green color of chlorophyll]

Add these functions to the tomato plant diagram.

2. Point out that plants are adapted for surviving in many different environments and that the shapes and textures of their leaves are clues for understanding how they capture light while overcoming the dangers that surround them. Farmers have also selected and bred edible plants for desirable properties related to taste and nutrition.

Reflecting on the Investigation

1. Distribute the other demonstration plants and encourage students to compare the shapes, textures, and odors of leaves. Ask what leaf properties farmers may be selecting for.

2. Direct the children to write what they have learned in their journals. Provide some questions as prompts for further reflection:

   ❀ *How does the way plants get food compare to the way animals, including humans, get food?* [plants make food; animals eat plants or other animals that eat plants]

❀ *Why are plants important to life on earth?* [provide food for animals; make oxygen; absorb carbon dioxide]

❀ *What leaves do you eat?*

❀ *What is something interesting you learned about leaves?*

Going Further

Leaf Math: Area and Perimeter
❀ Students trace the outlines of several kinds of edible leaves with different shapes and determine the <u>areas</u> and <u>perimeters</u> from the tracings. They then analyze and compare the two types of measurements to discover that perimeter (a linear measurement) is not related to area (a two-dimensional measurement).

Leaf Nutrition: Salad Greens Go Head to Head
❀ Have students compare the nutrients in romaine and iceberg lettuce. Ask, *Which lettuce leaves are highest in vitamins A and C? What other differences are there?* Add additional leaves such as spinach and chard for the greens comparison. You can find nutrition facts for fruits

and vegetables on the USDA Web site at *www.nal.usda.gov/fnic/foodcomp/search/* or by purchasing the Fresh Fruit and Vegetable Photo Cards from the California Department of Education's Educational Resources Catalog at *www.cde.ca.gov/re/pn/rc/*.

Leaf Science: Leaf Pigment Investigation

❀ "But my purple cabbage leaf isn't green!" Invite students to investigate the multiple pigments found in leaves. Show them how to use a simple process of paper <u>chromatography</u> described below) to separate and reveal the various leaf pigments.

Leaf Chromatography

What You Need
  ✳ leaves of different colors (red chard, spinach, amaranth)
  ✳ white coffee filters
  ✳ clear plastic drink cups with x-cut (straw) lids
  ✳ solvent: white vinegar or isopropyl alcohol

Paper Chromatography
1. Cut the coffee filters into strips approximately 1/2" wide and a little longer than a cup with the lid on it.

2. Pour 1/2" inch of solvent into a cup.

3. Using the edge of a penny, press a line of pigment from a leaf onto the filter strip, 1 inch from the end.

4. With a pencil, label the other end of the filter strip with the name of the plant.

5. Poke the labeled end of the strip up through the bottom of the lid's "x." Adjust the paper so that when you place the lid on the cup the lower end of the strip is in the solvent and the line of leaf pigment is suspended just above its surface.

6. Guide students in conducting this chromatography experiment for various leaves. Have them record and compare their observations. How many different plant pigments do they observe? Is there a pigment all the leaves have in common?

Leaf Language Arts and Social Studies: People Using Leaves

❀ Have students choose a leaf with an interesting use or history and write about it on large index cards, creating "fact cards." Some examples include papyrus for writing paper, pandanas for grass skirts and mats, tea leaves for beverages, and flax for linen. In addition, the class can post these on a world map to show where the uses originated.

Flowers

FLOWER FUNCTION: attract
pollinators to reproductive parts

Throughout history people have admired the amazing structures and characteristics of flowers, cultivating many plants especially for this part. In this lesson children taste and dissect edible flowers and explore the structures that enable plants to <u>reproduce</u>. The children also contribute to a pollination reenactment and learn how flower attributes attract pollinators.

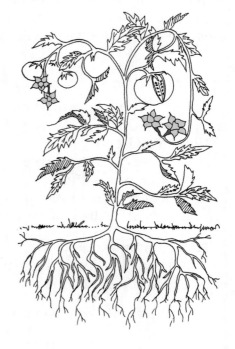

What You Need

Plant Snack Items (at least 4 cut pieces of each item per child)
* ✱ broccoli crowns
* ✱ cauliflower florets

Dissection Materials for Student Pairs
* ✱ 2 simple flowers (nasturtiums, primroses, or vinca)
* ✱ magnifier
* ✱ 2 paper plates
* ✱ 2 flat toothpicks
* ✱ journals
* ✱ pencils and crayons
* ✱ 30-centimeter ruler
* ✱ Flower Nutrition Labels (broccoli and cauliflower, p. 73)

For the Group
* ✱ uncut example of each snack item
* ✱ several extra flowers for dissection
* ✱ Parts of a Flower diagram (p. 67)
* ✱ pollinator puppet (bee, hummingbird, or butterfly)
* ✱ 2 paper model flowers for pollinator reenactment (optional)
* ✱ Structures of a Tomato Plant diagram (from Lesson 2)
* ✱ classroom board or chart paper
* ✱ marking pens
* ✱ snack supplies: cutting board, knife, containers, spoons, plates, and napkins
* ✱ additional flowers: choose a selection of edible fresh and dried flowers (see Plant Products Kit, p. 12, and Produce Shopping List by Lesson, p. 13)

Getting Ready

1. Collect or purchase simple flowers for dissection. Do not use composite flowers, like daisies, because many of the reproductive parts are reduced or missing. Select complete flowers that have an obvious pistil and stamens. Nasturtiums are ideal — they're edible and common in gardens. Vinca (also known as periwinkle) grows wild along streams and roadsides. Alstroemeria is available from most florists. Look for the presence of powdery pollen on its stamen.

2. Cut the broccoli and cauliflower into bite-sized pieces and make name labels for the plant snacks.

3. Just before the session, organize the dissecting materials, produce, and plants that students will taste.

4. Using the Parts of a Flower diagram, draw a cross section of a flower on the board and write the dissection tasks shown on the illustration (right).

1. Write <u>Flower</u>: <u>Nasturtium</u> and the date.
2. Observe and draw the whole flower.
3. Dissect the flower using a toothpick. Observe and count the parts.
4. Use a toothpick to open the ovary carefully and count the eggs.
5. Tape the flower parts into your journal and label them.

Tastings and Journals

1. Have children wash their hands and get out their journals. Refer to the Structures of a Tomato Plant diagram and encourage volunteers briefly to share what they have learned about plant structures thus far.

2. If students do not remember the functions of roots, stems, or leaves it may be useful to draw a small rain cloud near the tomato plant, and trace the path of the water into the soil, up through the roots and stem to other parts.

3. If necessary, review with students the procedures for observing, tasting, and recording their findings in their journals.

4. Hold up a broccoli crown. Ask,

   ❀ *What part of the plant do you think the dark green lumpy structures at the top represent?* [flower buds]

5. The broccoli crowns are clusters of unopened flower buds. Show students the cauliflower and explain that the two plants are closely related. Write "<u>Flower</u>" on the board and have students title and date their journal pages.

6. Distribute the Flower Nutrition Labels and ask partners to discuss what important nutrients they could get by eating these flowers. Encourage children to taste the raw samples and describe the flavors. Ask volunteers to share ways they have eaten broccoli or cauliflower prepared for meals.

Exploring Flower Characteristics

1. Distribute a flower to each student. Invite students to describe characteristics of flowers based on the ones in their hands and those they've encountered in the past. Encourage individuals to report properties that they experience through all of their senses and record their ideas.

   ❀ *What are flowers like?* [brightly colored, sweet smelling, stinky, delicate]

   ❀ *What do we call the brightly colored parts of a flower?* [petals]

2. Introduce the Parts of a Flower diagram and label the petals on your drawing. Have students examine the flower gently without taking it apart as you continue to identify and label the parts (stem, stamen, pollen, pistil, etc.). You will label remaining parts after the dissection.

Dissecting a Flower to Explore Structures

1. Tell the children the name of the simple flower they will be dissecting. Add the flower name to the board and journal drawings. Walk children through the dissection steps. Tell them to look for all the structures they've learned about.

2. As students dissect their flowers, point out that their flower may be different in several ways from the flower diagram. For instance, the pistil may be shorter and the number of stamens much greater.

3. Circulate among the students, assisting where needed in identifying parts and opening the pistil. Encourage them to add counts, measurements, and descriptive words to their flower drawings. They may try tasting the nasturtium nectar.

4. Revisit the Parts of a Flower diagram and have students assist you in labeling the remaining parts of your drawing on the board (ovary, ovules, nectar, etc.)

Pollinators at Work

1. Invite the children to think about flowers they have seen in gardens. Ask:

   ❀ *What kinds of living things have you seen around flowers?* [butterflies, bees, hummingbirds, ladybugs, dragonflies, ants, beetles, flies]

   ❀ *Why are these animals visiting a flower?* [looking for food — pollen, nectar, insects]

❀ *Why might a plant provide nectar as a sweet treat?* [to attract animals that will <u>pollinate</u> the flower — pollinators]

2. Explain that flowering plants need pollen from the stamen to be moved to the pistil to fertilize the ovules in order to make seeds. Most plants require pollen from a different flower or another plant of the same species. Since plants can't move, they rely on animals to transport the pollen for them.

3. Using the Parts of a Flower diagram or flower models and volunteers to animate the pollinator puppets, guide the children in enacting the following process of <u>pollination</u>:

   a. A flower has bright, sometimes scented <u>petals</u> that make it noticeable to animal pollinators passing by.

   b. Deep in the center of this flower is sweet sugary <u>nectar</u> that the flower makes to lure <u>pollinators</u>.

   c. As the pollinator enters the flower it bumps up against one of the <u>stamens</u>.

   d. *Does anyone know what the dusty stuff on the stamens is called?* [<u>pollen</u>] *Does anyone know someone who gets <u>allergies</u> when flowers release their pollen?*

   e. *What happens when the pollinator bumps up against the dusty stamen?* [It gets pollen on its body.]

   f. The pollinator flies away covered with pollen, then lands on a different flower, where it bumps up against the middle part of the flower, called the <u>pistil</u>.

   g. A pollen grain falls onto the top part of the pistil, called the stigma, and sprouts a long tube that grows down to the <u>ovary</u>. Inside the ovary are tiny <u>ovules</u>, each containing an even smaller <u>egg</u>. (Trace with your finger the path down the center of the pistil to the eggs inside the ovary.)

   h. Male sex cells, or sperm, from the pollen grain travel down the tube, enter an ovule, and <u>fertilize</u> the egg. When the egg is fertilized, the ovule then develops into a <u>seed</u>.

   i. As the pollinator goes from flower to flower, it picks up and drops off new pollen grains on new flowers, enabling the plants' eggs to be fertilized.

Flower Function Ideas Based on Observations

1. Have the children share their observations and ideas about the functions of a flower's structures:

   ❀ *What features do the petals have that might be helpful in getting the flower pollinated?* [colors, lines, spots, other markings leading towards the center of the flower where the nectar and pollen are located.]

These are sometimes referred to as <u>bee guides</u>.

❀ *Where did you see the tiny ovules?* [the ovary]

❀ The pistil contains the ovary and eggs.
Do you think this would be a male or female part of the plant? [female]

❀ *Where did you see the pollen?* [the stamen]

❀ The pollen fertilizes the eggs. *Do you think the pollen-covered stamen is a male or female part of the plant?* [male]

2. Explain that pollination is plant reproduction, involving male and female parts and creating offspring — the seed.

❀ *Why do you think plants have flowers?* [attract pollinators to transfer pollen to the pistil to fertilize eggs that will become seeds]

Reflecting on the Investigation

1. Add the flower functions to the Structures of a Tomato Plant diagram. [attract pollinators for reproduction] Direct the children to write what they've learned in their journals.

2. Provide some questions as prompts for further reflection.

❀ *What do you think would happen if all the flowers on a plant were picked?*

❀ *What would happen if a plant's pollinators became extinct?*

❀ *What pollinators have you seen?*

❀ *What other edible flowers have you sampled?*

3. Present the additional fresh and dried flower examples and see if students can identify reproductive parts.

Going Further

Flower Math: Counting Buds, Flowers, and Seed Pods

❀ When plants are flowering in the garden, take students out for a math challenge. Ask, *How many closed buds, open flowers, and seed pods (the fruit from flower ovaries) can you count on a plant?* After collecting data ask, *Is there a relationship between the size of the flower and the number of flowers on a plant? Between the size of the flower and the size of the seed pod?*

Flower Nutrition: Broccoli and Cauliflower
❀ Have students consider two flower vegetables. Broccoli is considered an excellent food source because it is high in so many nutrients. Both broccoli and cauliflower are cruciferous foods. Foods in this category are thought to help in the prevention of certain types of cancer. Ask, *What are some other cruciferous foods?* Continue an exploration of vegetable nutrition.

Flower Science: Pollinator Preference
❀ Encourage children to pose questions about the variety of shapes, sizes, smells, and colors that flowers come in. Ask, *Why might a flower be white?* [more easily visible for night-flying pollinators such as moths and bats] *Why might a flower be stinky?* [attracts flies and beetles] *Why might one flower have its parts laid out like a landing pad, while another has them tucked inside a tube of petals?* [nectar drinking method of bee versus hummingbird] Take children out to the garden to observe pollinators in action and find clues to pollinator preferences.

Flower Cooking and Social Science: Tea Party
❀ Many cultures prepare teas from plants, and flowers are common ingredients. Flowers are also used in other prepared foods. Involve your students and their parents in a tea party to celebrate flowers. Add dried lavender blossoms to sugar cookies for a delightful accent. Add violets, pansies, or calendula petals to finger sandwiches or spring rolls. Jasmine or hibiscus tea will complete the flower theme.

Flower Language Arts: The Unicorn's Garden
❀ Now that children have begun thinking about the many forms flowers take, ask them to invent an imaginary flower that grows in a magical garden. Have them describe the flower in their journals and how it attracts a special make-believe pollinator.

Fruits

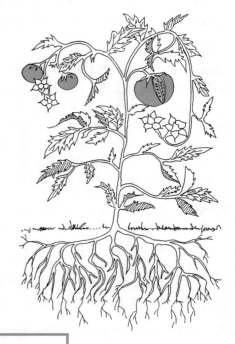

FRUIT FUNCTIONS: hold and protect seeds; attract animals for seed dispersals

Children draw, dissect, and analyze their findings about two kinds of fruits of the same size. First they examine and estimate the number of seeds in a cherry tomato. They count the actual number and contribute the data to a class chart. Next, they dissect a large grape and count its seeds. They then analyze the data from both seed counts. Students compare the structures of fruits, which hold and protect the seeds and contribute to seed dispersal.

What You Need

Plant Snack Items (at least 4 cut pieces of each item per child)

 ✳ red and green bell pepper pieces
 ✳ grapes and cherry tomatoes (taste after dissection)

Dissection Materials for Student Pairs

 ✳ cherry tomato
 ✳ grape with seeds
 ✳ 4 flat toothpicks
 ✳ magnifier
 ✳ paper plate or cutting board
 ✳ dissection knives
 ✳ journals
 ✳ pencils and crayons
 ✳ Fruit Nutrition Labels (red and green bell peppers, p. 74)

> The tomatoes and grapes with seeds should be as close to the same size as possible. Globe grapes work well.

For the Group

 ✳ 1/2 red and 1/2 green bell pepper
 ✳ 1 large tomato
 ✳ What Fruits and Vegetables Do I Eat Chart
 ✳ How Many Seeds in a Tomato/Grape Chart
 ✳ Structures of a Tomato Plant diagram (from Lesson 2)
 ✳ Parts of a Flower diagram (p. 67)
 ✳ 11"x 2" paper sentence strips and tape
 ✳ classroom board or chart paper
 ✳ marking pens
 ✳ snack supplies: cutting board, knife, containers, spoons, plates, and napkins
 ✳ additional fruits: include those that are customarily called vegetables, such as squash and cucumbers (see Plant Products Kit, p. 12, and Produce Shopping List by Lesson, p. 13)

Getting Ready

1. Prepare the produce for tasting and dissection. Reserve some tomatoes and grapes for the students to taste after the dissection. Red bell peppers are very high in vitamins C and A, and have a sweet tangy taste that most people enjoy. Prepare a smaller quantity of green bell pepper pieces (which have significantly less of vitamins C and A) so that children can compare the unripe and mature fruits. Keep half a red and half a green pepper intact, with seeds revealed.

2. Just before the session, organize the produce, fruits, and dissecting materials that students will need.

3. Draw the How Many Seeds in a Tomato/Grape chart on the board with the headings "# of Seeds in a Tomato" and "# of Seeds in a Grape."

4. Write the steps shown on the illustration (right) on your board to guide the children's dissection.

1. Write <u>Fruit</u>: <u>Tomato</u>, <u>Grape</u>, and the date.
2. Observe and draw the whole fruit.
3. Draw a line where you will bisect the tomato.
4. Observe and draw the inside of the tomato.
5. Write down your estimate of the number of seeds.
6. Use a toothpick to count the seeds.
7. Write the actual number of seeds counted.
8. Repeat these steps with the grape.

What Fruits and Vegetables Do I Eat?

1. Have children take out their journals and prepare for the tastings. Using the Structures of a Tomato Plant diagram, review the plant parts and functions that have been covered so far.

2. Post the What Fruits and Vegetables Do I Eat Chart and pose the question. Once everyone has responded and you have recorded a broad variety, ask the children to use their botany knowledge to identify the plant parts among the vegetables on the list. Label each food with a part as students identify it. For instance, next to "carrot" write "root" and next to "collards" write "leaves." You will inevitably come across items such as cucumber, zucchini, and tomato. *What parts of a plant are these?*

3. Have the children consider the fruits on your list. Ask what they all have in common.

   ❀ *If you were to cut the fruits open, what would they all have inside?* [seeds]

   ❀ *Which of our vegetables have seeds inside? What part of the plant are they?* [the fruit]

4. Explain that the word "<u>vegetable</u>" is a culinary or kitchen term, not a botanical word. As students can see from their list, a vegetable can be an item from almost any part of the plant. Although the word "fruit" is used in the kitchen, as well, it is also a botanical word that describes a part of the plant. Ask,

   ❀ *How do we know if something is botanically a <u>fruit</u>?* [contains seeds]

Tastings and Journals

1. Display the red and green bell peppers that you cut in half and ask what part of the plant they represent. Confirm the identification of fruit, and have students title their journal page "Fruit" and record the date.

2. Review with students the Parts of a Flower diagram and the process of pollination. Draw their attention to the ovary and ovules that become seeds. Ask,

   ❀ *What part of the flower became the fruit? Why?* [the ovary; it contains the seeds]

3. Explain that these are sweet bell peppers and not hot chili peppers. Ask students for ideas explaining why one pepper is red and the other is green. Accept all suggestions, then provide the additional information that almost all peppers start off green. In fact, both samples are the same kind of bell pepper — the green one was picked earlier, while the red one remained on the plant longer to mature and ripen.

4. As they snack, have pairs discuss the information on the Fruit Nutrition Labels and consider why the peppers might taste differently.

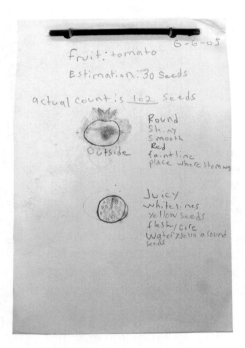

Dissecting Fruits to Explore Structures

1. Announce that today students will be dissecting and comparing two fruits that are important to people around the world: tomatoes and grapes.

2. Review the dissection steps and direct student pairs to begin with the tomato, making careful drawings of the outside of the fruit, including where it was attached to the plant.

3. After pairs cut open their tomatoes, have them <u>estimate</u> how many seeds they think are in them and record the number in their journal as "Estimate of Seeds = ___."

> Tell the children that it is OK and expected that their estimates and the actual number of seeds they count do not exactly match.

4. Show students how to use toothpicks to separate and count the slippery tomato seeds. Encourage them to look closely at the seeds.

   ❀ *Are they all the same size?*

   ❀ *How are the seeds attached to the inside of the fruit?*

   ❀ *What might be the advantage to having a jelly-like substance around the seeds?* [protects them]

5. Working together, have each pair count the seeds. Discuss possible strategies they might use for counting large numbers of seeds, such as keeping a tally, grouping into 5 or 10 seeds, and counting seeds in half of the tomato and then multiplying by two.

6. Visit pairs to assist with the cuts and counting. Have them record in their journal the number of seeds they counted as "Seeds Counted = ___."

7. Have pairs record the number of tomato seeds they counted on the class chart and collect a grape to dissect. Tell them to repeat the steps of estimation, observing, drawing, counting, and recording data for the grape.

Analyzing Tomato and Grape Data

1. Tell the group they will now <u>analyze</u> the seed count data. Begin with the tomato data by asking volunteers to help you identify and circle the largest number of seeds counted and the smallest number. Have them determine the <u>range</u> by finding the difference (subtraction) between these two numbers.

2. With the children's help, rewrite the numbers of seeds counted in order from smallest to largest. For example: 12, 17, 22, 22, 31, 45, 48, 49, 50, 64.

3. Distribute sentence strips and give each pair a few minutes to agree on and write one or two true statements about the data. Rotate among the pairs, discussing and (if necessary) modifying the statements to improve accuracy. Post the statements. Possible responses include:
   – The range is 52 (64 minus 12).
   – Two people counted 22 seeds.
   – The class counted a total of 360 tomato seeds.
   – The average number counted was 36.
   – 3 tomatoes had seed numbers in the 40s.

4. Ask children to consider their estimates of tomato seeds. Ask, *How many people estimated higher than their count? How many had low estimates? Looking at the group data, what count would you estimate for this uncut tomato that is about the same size as the other tomatoes? What would you estimate for this large tomato?*

5. Repeat this approach with the grape data. The seed counts and range will be quite small, something like: 0, 1, 1, 2, 2, 2, 4, 4, 4, 6. These big differences in seed numbers can prompt an interesting discussion about reproduction in tomatoes versus grapes.

Fruit Function Ideas Based on Observations

6. Direct students to think about what they observed and learned as they examined the various fruits. Ask,

   ❀ *What was similar about both the tomato and grape?* [round; jelly-like and moist inside; seeds inside]

   ❀ *Why do animals like to eat fruit?* [tastes sweet, juicy]

❀ *When an animal eats a fruit with seeds inside, what often happens to the seeds?* [they are not digested and are deposited with the animal's scat]

Through animals, seed is distributed away from the parent plant (so new plants don't compete for resources), along with a package of natural fertilizer (the scat).

2. Add the fruit functions to the Structures of a Tomato Plant diagram and ask,

❀ *In what ways are fruits important to plants?* [they hold and protect the seeds; they taste good to animals that eat them and disperse seeds]

Reflecting on the Investigation

1. Bring out the tastings of tomatoes and grapes. Have students compare them to other fruit examples in the Plant Products Kit. See if they can find old flower parts on a pomegranate, apple, or other fruit. Challenge them to find undeveloped or infertile seeds in items such as bananas, zucchini, or "seedless" fruits such as watermelon. Save some seed samples and revisit them in the next lesson.

2. Have students write in their journals about the results of their dissection and seed counts. Ask them to include at least two questions that spark their curiosity about fruits.

Going Further

Fruit Math: Symmetry and Tomato Algebra

❀ The seeds inside fruits are often arranged in symmetrical patterns. Cut additional fruit examples from the lesson in half and compare the two halves for symmetry.

❀ *How many tomato plants should be grown to provide every student at school with one tomato?* To help solve the problem, have students determine approximately how many tomatoes grow on one plant and how many students are at the school. If there are 12 tomatoes on one plant and 500 students, the algebraic equation to solve for *x* (the number of plants needed) looks like this:

(tomatoes on 1 plant) multiplied by x = (number of students) or
12x = 500, x = number of tomato plants needed

BOTANY ON YOUR PLATE

Fruit Nutrition: Red vs. Green Bell Peppers

❀ Using the Fruit Nutrition Labels have students compare the nutrients in red and green bell peppers. Ask, *Which fruit is highest in vitamins A and C? Why might farmers pick bell peppers when they are green? How do prices compare for red and green peppers? After a green bell pepper is picked, how does it change if it is not refrigerated?*

Fruit Ethnobotany and Social Science: Crop Varieties

❀ For thousands of years farmers have selected for different traits to enhance the taste or utility of different plant crops. Invite students to make their own comparisons between different varieties of the same fruit such as apples, pears, grapes, tomatoes, and squash and share their ratings. Try including heirloom varieties along with more common commercial ones. Extend this topic to explore issues of crop <u>diversity</u> and its importance for disease resistance, adaptability, and species health.

Fruit Cooking and Language Arts: So Many Salsa Recipes!

❀ Students can create their own salsa blends and recipe cards by combining ingredients from a "salsa bar" they help prepare. Popular produce selections include: tomatoes, tomatillos, strawberries, oranges, mangos, pineapples, cilantro, green onions, basil, and chiles or sweet peppers. Have students identify which items in the salsa bar are fruits and which are other parts of a plant.

Seeds

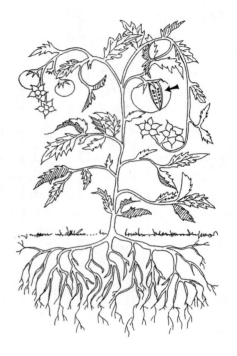

SEED FUNCTIONS: hold embryo; store food for baby plant

Children dissect and compare bean and almond seeds. They observe the tiny plant embryos surrounded by food for the baby plant, and test the seeds for the presence of natural oil. They learn to use a <u>Venn diagram</u> to organize their seed observations.

What You Need

Plant Snack Items (at least 4 cut pieces of each item per child)
* almonds or sunflower seeds
* hummus and/or chickpeas (garbanzo beans)
* whole grain bread with visible grains and seeds

Dissection Materials for Student Pairs
* 2 raw almonds
* 2 green fava or lima beans
* magnifier
* paper plates or cutting board
* sturdy metal spoon
* brown paper bag cut into 2"x 4" pieces
* journals
* pencils and crayons
* Seed Nutrition Labels (chickpea and sunflower, p. 75)

For the Group
* unprocessed examples of each snack item
* several whole bean pods
* raw peanuts in the shell
* clear plastic tape
* Inside a Fava Bean and Inside an Almond Seed diagrams (p. 68)
* Venn diagram on classroom board or chart paper
* Structures of a Tomato Plant diagram (from Lesson 2)
* marking pens
* snack supplies: cutting board, knife, containers, spoons, plates, and napkins
* additional seeds: include fresh seeds such as snap peas or soy beans (edamame) in pods and dry seeds such as grains (see Plant Products Kit, p. 12, and Produce Shopping List by Lesson, p. 13)

Getting Ready

1. Purchase the produce and plant snack items. If possible obtain fresh fava or lima beans, otherwise soak large white, dry lima beans overnight. The larger the beans, the easier it is for children to observe the plant embryo.

2. Cut slices of bread into halves or quarters. Hummus is a nutritious dip that originated in the Middle East and is traditionally made from chickpeas (also called garbanzo beans), ground sesame seeds (tahini), lemon juice, and garlic.

3. Purchase a few dozen unsalted peanuts in the shell for students to observe but not eat. **Note:** While peanuts are ideal for viewing the embryo, they cause serious allergic reactions in many people. To eliminate this hazard, carefully open the peanuts in an area not used by students. Wash your hands to remove peanut dust then wrap each pair of peanuts in clear packing tape so that the embryo is visible. Put clear tape around some peanuts in the shell so that children can also observe the fruit pod.

4. Just before the session, organize the snack items, the dissection materials, and the plants that students will dissect.

5. Post the Structures of a Tomato Plant diagram, and draw a large Venn diagram on the board. Have the pieces of brown paper bag on hand; students will use them for a "squash" test.

6. Draw a cross section of a seed on the board using the Inside a Fava Bean diagram and write the tasks (shown right) on the board to guide the dissection.

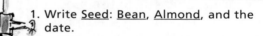

1. Write <u>Seed</u>: <u>Bean</u>, <u>Almond</u>, and the date.
2. Observe and draw the outside of the seeds.
3. Open the bean and draw the embryo.
4. Open the almond and draw the embryo.
5. Draw and fill out the Venn diagram.

Tastings and Journals

1. Have children get ready for the tastings and take out their journals. Review the Structures of a Tomato Plant diagram and have volunteers describe the plant parts and functions they have studied.

2. Display the bread and ask what part of the plant they think the food was made from. [seeds] Stimulate a discussion about the ingredients of bread. Connect the ingredients with the terms "seed," "grain," and "flour." If possible, show examples of whole grains such as wheat.

3. Show the chickpeas to help students identify a seed, and have them title their journal page "<u>Seed</u>" and record the date.

4. Encourage students to taste and describe the seed foods to a partner, and document their findings in their journals. Invite them to share knowledge they may have about the cultural origins and nutritional values of these foods.

Dissecting Seeds to Explore Structures

1. Announce that today students will be looking at two kinds of seeds, a bean and a <u>nut</u>. Show children the bean <u>pod</u> with beans inside, and prompt them to note that the pod is the fruit that contains the seeds. Explain that the hard covering around the almond seed is called the shell. When on the tree, the shell is enclosed in a fleshy pod — the fruit.

2. Draw children's attention to the clear <u>seed coat</u> of the bean and the brown, papery covering of the almond. Using a fingernail, demonstrate how to break open the seeds into two equal halves. One half will have the embryo still attached.

3. Distribute the two seeds and have students begin by drawing the outside of each seed, then opening the seeds and observing their insides.

4. Encourage students to use magnifiers to look for evidence of a baby plant, called an <u>embryo</u>. Surrounding the embryo is stored food in the form of the <u>cotyledon</u>. Circulate among student pairs, asking questions about what they are observing and checking that they label their findings.

5. When everyone has documented their dissections, tell the students they will use a "squash" test to compare the composition of the two seeds. Demonstrate how to use a sturdy metal spoon to crush an almond and a bean on a piece of brown paper bag. Firmly rub the crushed seeds into the paper until you've created a mark. Label the marks and compare their qualities. [The almond leaves an oily stain, the bean mark is wet but not oily.] For young students, conduct this as a demonstration.

Seed Function Ideas Based on Observations

1. As a group, ask pairs to share their findings from the dissection. Ask:
   - ❧ *What was inside the seed?* [a baby plant]
   - ❧ *What made you think it was an embryo or baby plant?* [it had tiny leaves and a root]
   - ❧ *What do you think the rest of the seed surrounding the embryo is for?* [stored food for the embryo; protects the embryo]

2. Introduce the Venn diagram and have students draw it in their journals. Tell them to find three <u>attributes</u> or ways that the almond and fava bean are different and three ways they are similar and fill out their Venn diagram. (If your class is not familiar with Venn diagrams they can make two lists.)

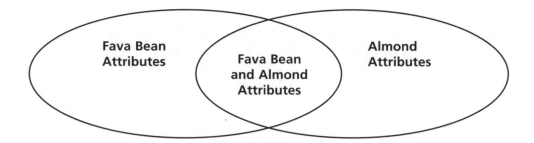

Fava Bean
Attributes

Fava Bean
and Almond
Attributes

Almond
Attributes

3. Guide the students in sharing their findings. During the discussion, record their responses in the Venn diagram on the board.

❀ *What are some differences you noticed between the almond and the bean?* [color, size, wet/dry, watery/oily, soft/hard]

❀ *What are some similarities you saw?* [both have seed coats, both have embryos, both come from a fruit with a shell or pod]

4. Distribute the plastic-covered peanuts for comparison. Ask volunteers to look for similarities to the bean and almond while you list their findings on the board. *What evidence is there that the peanut is a seed?*

Reflecting on the Investigation

1. Draw students' attention to their list of attributes shared by seeds. Provide some questions or prompts for their reflection about seeds.

❀ *In what ways are seeds important to plants?* [hold and feed baby plant/embryo to create new plants]

❀ *In what ways are seeds important to people?* [edible; create new plants for food and oxygen]

❀ *What might happen if, all of a sudden, tomato plants couldn't make seeds?* [tomato plants would become extinct]

❀ *What is something interesting you learned about seeds?*

2. Add the seed functions to the Structures of a Tomato Plant diagram and have students write in their journals about the results of their seed comparisons.

3. Direct the children to think about and share what they have learned as they examine other examples of seeds.

Going Further

Seed Math: Planting

❀ From using seed spacing guides on seed packets to figuring out how to divide the garden bed, planting activities are full of math opportunities. Help children learn how to use their own bodies as measuring tools by measuring in hand-spans and paces. Explore fractions by having children divide beds of various shapes and sizes. Solve volume equations by having them determine how much <u>compost</u> to add.

Seed Nutrition and Cooking: Beans, Seeds, and Nuts

❀ Starting with chickpeas and sunflower seeds, have students compare the nutrients in a variety of seeds, nuts, and beans. *Which ones are highest in protein, fiber, and oil?*

❀ Involve the class in making a trail mix with a variety of dried fruits, nuts, and seeds to celebrate the harvest.

Seed Science: Sprouting

❀ Have students conduct <u>germination</u> studies of various kinds of seeds. They can make their own seed-starting cups and plant herbs to take home. Select seeds from <u>monocots</u> and <u>dicots</u> and invite students to compare the seed leaves or cotyledons of the germinating plants.

Seed Social Science: Wheat and Chickpeas

❀ Wheat, the primary grain in bread, was cultivated by people living in the region known as the Fertile Crescent as early as 9,000 years ago. Today much of this early farming region, which includes part of Turkey, Israel, Iraq, and Iran, has become desert. Chickpeas, or garbanzo beans, were first cultivated in the Mediterranean Basin 7,000 years ago, and spread to Ethiopia and India, eventually becoming the most widely consumed legume in the world. Have students choose a seed crop and research its origin and use by humans over time.

Seed Language Arts: Seed Adventure Stories

❀ Invite students to write adventure stories of a seed's journey from the fruit on its parent plant to its new home, and its development into a new plant. Remind them that animal characters, travel, environmental features, and events of nature may contribute to an exciting tale.

Plants — Top to Bottom

After first predicting which plant snacks will be eaten the most, children record their own selections and then analyze the class data. Next, they compare the results of this food preference study to the results from the same study in Lesson 1. In a guided discussion, children examine the results of the food study and propose ideas for sharing what they know with family and friends.

Throughout this unit, students have explored different ways that people use plants in various cultures. Referring back to the How Do People Use Plants Chart (from Lesson 1), extend the discussion to include the importance of plants to all life on earth. To end the lesson, have young botanists draw and write their reflections about plants in their journals.

What You Need

Plant Snack Items (at least 4 cut pieces of each item per child)
Choose the same snack items, representing each of the six parts of a plant, that you used in Lesson 1:
  ✳ carrots or jicama (roots)
  ✳ asparagus, kohlrabi, or broccoli stems (stems)
  ✳ celery, spinach, or red cabbage (leaves)
  ✳ broccoli crowns, cauliflower, or nasturtiums (flowers)
  ✳ red bell pepper, cucumber, cherry tomatoes, or raisins (fruits)
  ✳ almonds or fresh, shelled beans (seeds)

For Each Child
  ✳ journal
  ✳ pencil and crayons

For the Group
  ✳ uncut examples the plants used for snacks
  ✳ paper or index cards
  ✳ 11"x 2" paper sentence strips and tape
  ✳ Food Preference Study 2 Chart (new)
  ✳ Food Preference Study Chart (from Lesson 1)
  ✳ How Do People Use Plants Chart

* What Plants Do I Eat Chart (from Lesson 1)
* marking pens
* snack supplies: cutting board, knife, containers, spoons, plates, and napkins

Getting Ready

1. Wash and cut the produce and make a name card for each plant snack item.

2. Just before the session, arrange the plant snack buffet, name cards, plates, and napkins for easy access. Post the Food Preference Study 2 Chart and date it.

3. Have students wash their hands and place their journals nearby.

Tastings and Journals: Food Preference Study

1. Announce that today students will conduct a new food preference study. Tell them you have prepared enough plant snacks for everyone to have as many as four pieces of each food. Caution them to take only what they plan to eat.

2. Introduce each food featured in the snack buffet. Have children write the plant names in their journals as you list them on the Food Preference Study 2 Chart. (Leave enough room next to the plant names to add each child's data later in the lesson.) Ask children to under-line in their journal the food they predict will be eaten by the most people.

3. Explain that as in the first food preference study, one goal is to discover more about the group's food preferences, while encouraging everyone to try new foods. Ask students to describe the foods to their partners, and to include the new information they have gained about each one from previous lessons.

4. As they snack, have students keep a tally by making a mark next to the plant name of each item they eat. (Review tallying if necessary.)

5. Direct students to write and draw their observations in their journals, and record the total number of pieces of each food item they have eaten. As they finish, have them come to the board with their journals and contribute their totals to the Food Preference Study 2 Chart.

Which Plants Were Eaten the Most and Least?

1. Invite children to suggest ways to determine which foods were eaten most and least. Have them consider the list of class totals on the board. Depending on the grade level of your students, there are a number of approaches you can take — you want students to practice their math reasoning skills within the time constraints of the session.

2. Encourage students to discuss their ideas for most and least with each other, just as scientists discuss findings with their colleagues. Students may decide to compare piece totals, averages, or the number of zeros (indicating *not eaten* by a person) for each food. Give the class about five minutes to consider the evidence and to write their conclusions in their journals, then have students report their results.

3. Ask how their predictions about the food eaten by the most people compared with the results.

Revisiting the First Food Preference Study

1. Post the results of the first food preference study. Ask students to discuss similarities and differences between the two surveys.

2. Distribute sentence strips to pairs of students and have them write true statements about the two sets of data.

3. Post the true statements and facilitate a class discussion about the results and food experiences students have had since embarking on the curriculum.

   ❀ *Were there any foods that were eaten by more people after the* Botany on Your Plate *lessons than before?*

   ❀ *Was there a change in which food was eaten by the most people?*

   ❀ *Was there a change in the food* you *ate the most of?*

   ❀ *Have you noticed a change in the foods you like to eat?*

   ❀ *Have you encouraged a friend or family member to try a new food from plants?*

Revisiting the Plant Charts

1. Post the original What Plants Do I Eat Chart and encourage children to add new foods and correct the information based on their new knowledge. Use a different color marking pen to add to and modify the list. As you review the extended list, encourage children to tell you what plant part each item is and record it next to the item.

2. Post the original How Do People Use Plants Chart. Have children think back to previous lessons and add any new suggestions.

3. One primary use of plants that students have learned about is that

they provide us with food that we eat to generate energy. Ask, *Where do we get energy for other things like cars and homes?*

4. Share this story: Millions of years ago — before the dinosaurs — plants were capturing the sun's energy, converting it into food, and making more plant material. As the plants died, the plant matter piled up in places such as swamps and bogs where it was unable to break down. These layers of plant debris were covered by sediment. Time and massive pressure deep underground transformed the plant material into what we now call fossil fuels: oil, coal, and gas. When we use these resources we are burning the captured energy of ancient plants.

5. Discussion about energy derived from plants may lead to the topic of alternative sources of energy, such as biofuel made from crops. The search for alternative energy is driven by problems resulting from burning fossil fuels, which adds carbon dioxide to the air and contributes to global warming.

6. Have the students think back to the leaf lesson. Ask, *Name something on our planet that can take carbon dioxide out of the air?* [plants] Through photosynthesis, plants "clean" the air, extracting carbon dioxide and releasing oxygen. Plants' ability to make carbon-based food with the sun's energy, and to release oxygen is the basis of all life on earth.

Reflecting on Botany on Your Plate Investigations

1. Direct children to write in their journals about their experiences of studying edible plants. Provide some prompts for their reflection:

   ❀ *Describe two of your favorite activities.*

   ❀ *What plant foods would you recommend your friends try? Why?*

   ❀ *What edible plants do you plan to eat more of in the future? Why?*

   ❀ *How did your plant investigations change your understanding of how plants grow?*

   ❀ *What is the most important thing you learned about plants?*

Going Further

Plant Math: A Plant Study

❀ Have students select and draw their favorite garden plant. Help them decide on data to collect in an ongoing study of their plant. Help them form questions that will guide the study, such as how tall, how wide, or how fast their plant will grow. Give students time at regular intervals over several weeks to collect data and record their findings in their journals.

Plant Nutrition: Eating a Rainbow

❀ The color of a fruit or vegetable often corresponds to its micronutrients (vitamins, minerals, antioxidants). These micronutrients are important for the body in many ways. For instance, orange is associated with vitamin A, which is essential for healthy eyesight. Red often

History of Plant Science: How Plant Studies have Changed our Understanding (for grades 3 & 4)

Botanists once thought that nutrients and water from the soil made up most of the "bodies" of plants or trees that you see growing. Studies of how people think reveal that this is still a common misconception today.

1. Ask students to suggest observations that could support the idea that plants are made mostly of material from the soil.

2. List their ideas. [plants grow in soil; roots suck up water and nutrients; small soil particles cling to roots; nuts and seeds are hard like soil; plants grow better when fertilizer is added to soil; plants die when they are pulled from the soil]

3. Explain that in the 1900's, experiments using precise laboratory equipment revealed that only tiny amounts of minerals and soil nutrients make their way into a plant's structure over its lifetime. Most plants need these trace amounts for good growth, much as we need vitamins to stay healthy, but they can survive and even grow for a time without any new nutrients.

4. Point out that this discovery generated lots of scientific research to find answers to the following question:

   ❀ *If most material in a plant doesn't come from the soil, where does it come from?* [made by the plant through photosynthesis]

5. Invite students to develop a hydroponic research experiment to measure plant growth without soil.

indicates the presence of lycopene, which is associated with maintaining a healthy heart. Conduct a class study of food colors and their benefits. Culminate the study with a "rainbow roll-up" feast, using tortillas, a dressing or spread, and a food buffet that includes each color.

Plant Science: Changes in Understanding
❀ As scientists study something, their understanding of how it works often changes. See the box (p. 64) for a description of how botanists studying plants changed our understanding of how a plant grows. Have students write in their journals about how their understanding of plants has changed so far.

Plant Social Science and Gardening: Cultural Farming Techniques
❀ People of different cultures have discovered effective ways of farming in different environments. For example, Native Americans of the southwest developed a farming technique called "three sisters." They discovered that when corn, beans, and squash were planted together, the harvest was far greater than when the plants were each grown in separate plots. The corn provided a structure for bean vines to grow up; the beans enriched the soil with nitrogen; and the squash leaves shaded the surface of the soil, conserving moisture. Many cultures use another technique called "terraced farming" to increase crop yields in sloping terrain. Still other cultures developed a "raised-mound" technique to grow crops on rocky, infertile soil. Explore farming and gardening techniques from around the world.

Plant Language Arts and Social Science: Historical Figures and Poetry
❀ Find books for your class featuring people connected to plants who have made significant contributions to their communities. Such figures might include George Washington Carver and Cesar Chavez.

❀ The Japanese art of haiku very often uses references from nature. Have students write haikus that feature plant imagery.

Structures of a Tomato Plant

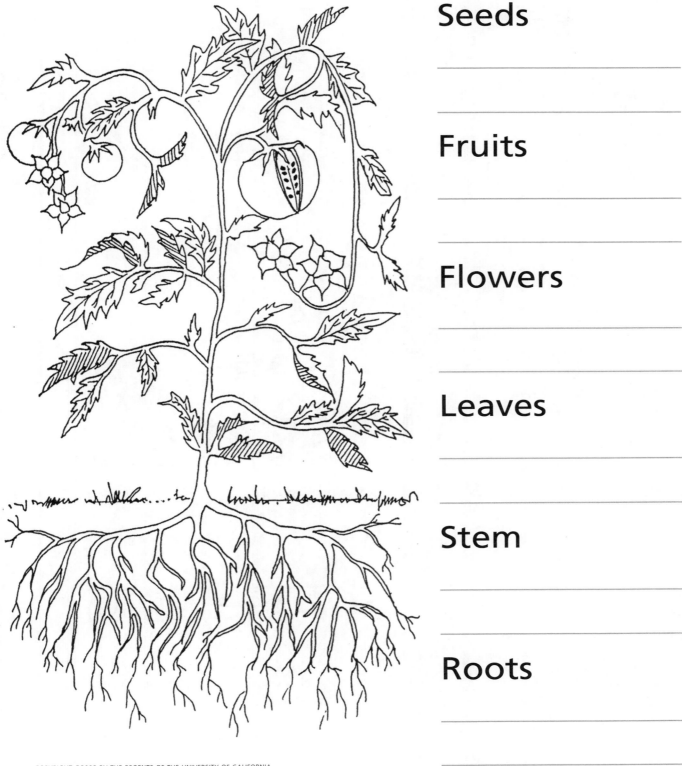

Seeds

_____

Fruits

_____

Flowers

_____

Leaves

_____

Stem

_____

Roots

_____

Photosynthesis

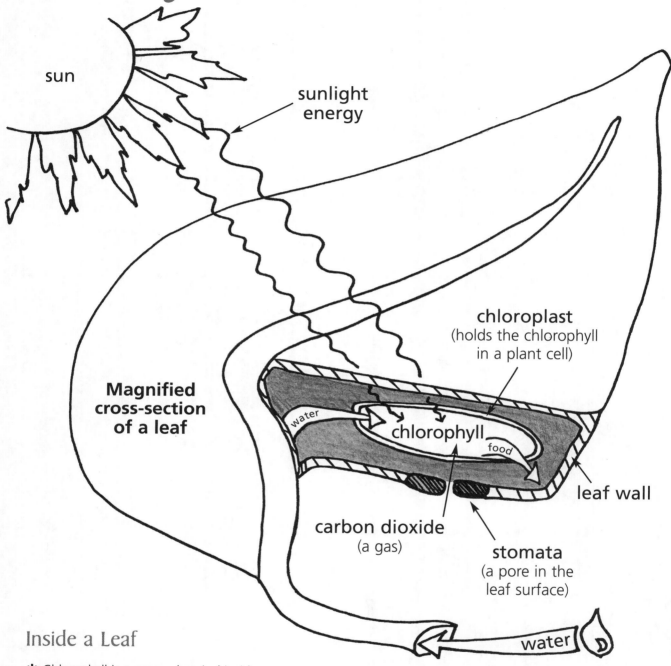

sun

sunlight energy

Magnified cross-section of a leaf

chloroplast
(holds the chlorophyll
in a plant cell)

water

chlorophyll

food

leaf wall

carbon dioxide
(a gas)

stomata
(a pore in the
leaf surface)

water

Inside a Leaf

✳ Chlorophyll is a green chemical inside
a plant cell that captures energy from sunlight.

✳ Chlorophyll enables the plant to make food in the form of carbohydrates from sunlight, water, and a gas
called carbon dioxide: **sunlight + water + carbon dioxide = food**

Parts of a Nasturtium Flower

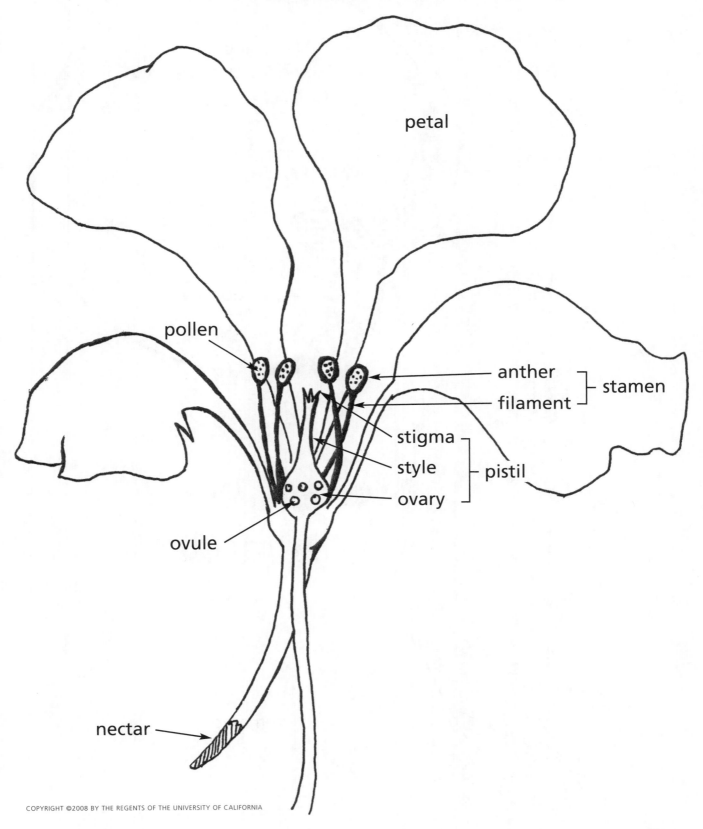

petal

pollen

anther

filament

stamen

stigma

style

pistil

ovary

ovule

nectar

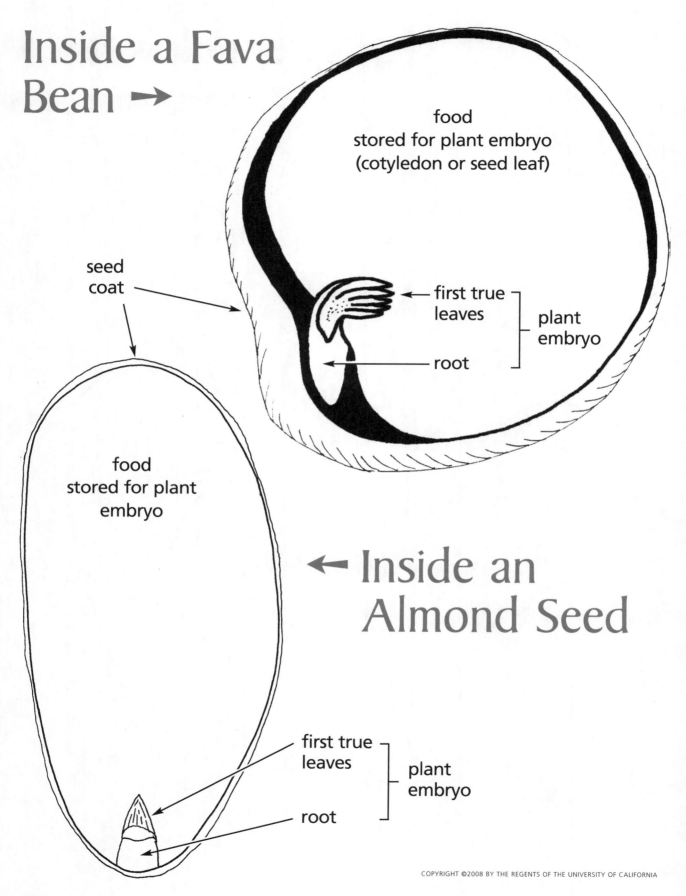

Inside a Fava Bean ➡

food
stored for plant embryo
(cotyledon or seed leaf)

seed
coat

first true
leaves

plant
embryo

root

food
stored for plant
embryo

⬅ Inside an Almond Seed

first true
leaves

plant
embryo

root

How to Read a Nutrition Facts Label

The following pages contain the nutrition labels for the lessons in this book. Before using the labels in the lessons, use the example on this page to review with students the components found on a label and how the percentages of nutrients relate to healthy intake.

Serving sizes are often smaller than the portion we actually eat. Read carefully!

Sometimes there is more than one serving in a package.

This food has a total of 230 calories per serving and 135 of them come from fat.

The **% Daily Value** column tells you how much of the daily recommended amount of a nutrient this food contains. (This is for the average person. See below for calorie need differences among people.)

The nutrients listed here, such as protein, are those considered highly important for the health of the average American.

In general, one should **limit** certain types of fat, cholesterol, and sodium, and make sure to **get enough** fiber, vitamins, and minerals. For these nutrients, 5% is considered a low source, 20% or more is high.

Use this as a guide for planning. It shows limits for cholesterol, fats, and sodium, and recommended amounts of carbohydrates and fiber. The amount of calories needed by each person depends on many factors, including age, gender, and activity level.

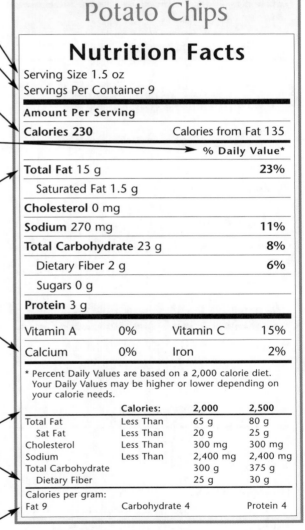

Potato Chips

Nutrition Facts

Serving Size 1.5 oz
Servings Per Container 9

Amount Per Serving

Calories 230   Calories from Fat 135

                                 % Daily Value*

Total Fat 15 g	**23%**
Saturated Fat 1.5 g	
Cholesterol 0 mg	
Sodium 270 mg	**11%**
Total Carbohydrate 23 g	**8%**
Dietary Fiber 2 g	**6%**
Sugars 0 g	
Protein 3 g	

Vitamin A	0%	Vitamin C	15%
Calcium	0%	Iron	2%

* Percent Daily Values are based on a 2,000 calorie diet. Your Daily Values may be higher or lower depending on your calorie needs.

	Calories:	2,000	2,500
Total Fat	Less Than	65 g	80 g
Sat Fat	Less Than	20 g	25 g
Cholesterol	Less Than	300 mg	300 mg
Sodium	Less Than	2,400 mg	2,400 mg
Total Carbohydrate		300 g	375 g
Dietary Fiber		25 g	30 g

Calories per gram:
Fat 9   Carbohydrate 4   Protein 4

You can calculate the amount of calories in a food that come from fat, carbohydrate, or protein using this information. For example:

    4 protein calories per gram x 3 grams of protein per serving = 12 calories from protein

Visit the *MyPyramid.gov* Web site for more nutrition information.

Root Nutrition Labels

Root Food Name:
CARROT
Zanahoria

Nutrition Facts

Serving Size	1 medium carrot

Amount Per Serving

Calories	33

% Daily Value*

Total Fat	0 g	
Saturated Fat	0 g	
Cholesterol	0 mg	
Sodium	25 mg	
Total Carbohydrate	7 g	
Dietary Fiber	3 g	**12%**
Sugars	3 g	
Protein	1 g	

Vitamin A	405%	Vitamin C	12%
Potassium	7%	Folic Acid	3%
Calcium	2%	Iron	2%

* Percent Daily Values are based on a 2,000 calorie diet. Your Daily Values may be higher or lower depending on your calorie needs.

This food was originally developed from wild plant species by people in this part of the world: **Central Asia**

Root Food Name:
JICAMA/YAMBEAN
Jicama

Nutrition Facts

Serving Size	1/2 cup sliced

Amount Per Serving

Calories	25

% Daily Value*

Total Fat	0 g	
Saturated Fat	0 g	
Cholesterol	0 mg	
Sodium	4 mg	
Total Carbohydrate	5 g	
Dietary Fiber	3 g	**12%**
Sugars	1 g	
Protein	1 g	

Vitamin A	0%	Vitamin C	20%
Potassium	3%	Folic Acid	2%
Calcium	1%	Iron	2%

* Percent Daily Values are based on a 2,000 calorie diet. Your Daily Values may be higher or lower depending on your calorie needs.

This food was originally developed from wild plant species by people in this part of the world: **Mexico/Central America**

Stem Nutrition Labels

ASPARAGUS

Stem Food Name:
ASPARAGUS
Espárrago

Nutrition Facts

Serving Size	6 medium spears

Amount Per Serving

Calories 27

		% Daily Value*
Total Fat 0 g		
Saturated Fat 0 g		
Cholesterol 0 mg		
Sodium 4 mg		
Total Carbohydrate 4 g		
Dietary Fiber 2 g		8%
Sugars 2 g		
Protein 2 g		

Vitamin A	15%	Vitamin C	30%
Potassium	8%	Folic Acid	23%
Calcium	2%	Iron	3%

* Percent Daily Values are based on a 2,000 calorie diet. Your Daily Values may be higher or lower depending on your calorie needs.

This food was originally developed from wild plant species by people in this part of the world: **Europe/Southern Asia**

KOHLRABI

Stem Food Name:
KOHLRABI
Colinabo

Nutrition Facts

Serving Size	1/2 cup sliced

Amount Per Serving

Calories 25

		% Daily Value*
Total Fat 0 g		
Saturated Fat 0 g		
Cholesterol 0 mg		
Sodium 17 mg		
Total Carbohydrate 5 g		
Dietary Fiber 1 g		4%
Sugars 2 g		
Protein 1 g		

Vitamin A	1%	Vitamin C	82%
Potassium	8%	Folic Acid	3%
Calcium	2%	Iron	2%

* Percent Daily Values are based on a 2,000 calorie diet. Your Daily Values may be higher or lower depending on your calorie needs.

This food was originally developed from wild plant species by people in this part of the world: **Europe**

Leaf Nutrition Labels

Leaf Food Name:
ROMAINE LETTUCE
Lechuga Romana

Nutrition Facts

Serving Size	1 cup torn

Amount Per Serving

Calories 9

% Daily Value*

Total Fat	0 g		
Saturated Fat	0 g		
Cholesterol	0 mg		
Sodium	4 mg		
Total Carbohydrate	2 g		
Dietary Fiber	1 g		**4%**
Sugars	1 g		
Protein	1 g		

Vitamin A	55%	Vitamin C	22%
Potassium	3%	Folic Acid	20%
Calcium	2%	Iron	3%

* Percent Daily Values are based on a 2,000 calorie diet. Your Daily Values may be higher or lower depending on your calorie needs.

This food was originally developed from wild plant species by people in this part of the world: **Southwest Asia/Europe**

Leaf Food Name:
ICEBERG LETTUCE
Lechuga Repollo

Nutrition Facts

Serving Size	1 cup torn

Amount Per Serving

Calories 7

% Daily Value*

Total Fat	0 g		
Saturated Fat	0 g		
Cholesterol	0 mg		
Sodium	6 mg		
Total Carbohydrate	1 g		
Dietary Fiber	1 g		**4%**
Sugars	1 g		
Protein	1 g		

Vitamin A	2%	Vitamin C	3%
Potassium	3%	Folic Acid	8%
Calcium	1%	Iron	2%

* Percent Daily Values are based on a 2,000 calorie diet. Your Daily Values may be higher or lower depending on your calorie needs.

This food was originally developed from wild plant species by people in this part of the world: **Southwest Asia/Europe**

Flower Nutrition Labels

BROCCOLI

Flower Food Name:
BROCCOLI
Bróculi

Nutrition Facts

Serving Size 1/2 cup chopped

Amount Per Serving

Calories 27

% Daily Value*

Total Fat 0 g		
Saturated Fat 0 g		
Cholesterol 0 mg		
Sodium 20 mg		
Total Carbohydrate 4 g		
Dietary Fiber 3 g		**12%**
Sugars 1 g		
Protein 2 g		

Vitamin A	22%	Vitamin C	97%
Potassium	7%	Folic Acid	10%
Calcium	4%	Iron	4%

* Percent Daily Values are based on a 2,000 calorie diet. Your Daily Values may be higher or lower depending on your calorie needs.

This food was originally developed from wild plant species by people in this part of the world: **Southern Europe**

CAULIFLOWER

Flower Food Name:
CAULIFLOWER
Coliflor

Nutrition Facts

Serving Size 1/2 cup chopped

Amount Per Serving

Calories 17

% Daily Value*

Total Fat 0 g		
Saturated Fat 0 g		
Cholesterol 0 mg		
Sodium 4 mg		
Total Carbohydrate 3 g		
Dietary Fiber 2 g		**8%**
Sugars 1 g		
Protein 1 g		

Vitamin A	2%	Vitamin C	57%
Potassium	8%	Folic Acid	10%
Calcium	2%	Iron	2%

* Percent Daily Values are based on a 2,000 calorie diet. Your Daily Values may be higher or lower depending on your calorie needs.

This food was originally developed from wild plant species by people in this part of the world: **Southern Europe**

Fruit Nutrition Labels

Fruit Food Name:

GREEN BELL PEPPER

Chile de Campana Verde

Nutrition Facts

Serving Size	1/2 cup chopped

Amount Per Serving

Calories	15	

% Daily Value*

Total Fat	0 g	
Saturated Fat	0 g	
Cholesterol	0 mg	
Sodium	1 mg	
Total Carbohydrate	3 g	
Dietary Fiber	1 g	**4%**
Sugars	1 g	
Protein	>1 g	

Vitamin A	6%	Vitamin C	75%
Potassium	3%	Folic Acid	3%
Calcium	0%	Iron	1%

* Percent Daily Values are based on a 2,000 calorie diet. Your Daily Values may be higher or lower depending on your calorie needs.

This food was originally developed from wild plant species by people in this part of the world: **Mexico/Central America**

Fruit Food Name:

RED BELL PEPPER

Chile de Campana Rojo

Nutrition Facts

Serving Size	1/2 cup chopped

Amount Per Serving

Calories	15	

% Daily Value*

Total Fat	0 g	
Saturated Fat	0 g	
Cholesterol	0 mg	
Sodium	1 mg	
Total Carbohydrate	3 g	
Dietary Fiber	1 g	**4%**
Sugars	3 g	
Protein	>1 g	

Vitamin A	57%	Vitamin C	160%
Potassium	3%	Folic Acid	3%
Calcium	0%	Iron	1%

* Percent Daily Values are based on a 2,000 calorie diet. Your Daily Values may be higher or lower depending on your calorie needs.

This food was originally developed from wild plant species by people in this part of the world: **Mexico/Central America**

Seed Nutrition Labels

Seed Food Name:
CHICKPEA
Garbanzo

Nutrition Facts

Serving Size	1/2 cup, cooked

Amount Per Serving

Calories	134

% Daily Value*

Total Fat	2 g	
Saturated Fat	0 g	
Cholesterol	0 mg	
Sodium	6 mg	
Total Carbohydrate	22 g	
Dietary Fiber	6 g	24%
Sugars	4 g	
Protein	6 g	

Vitamin A	0%	Vitamin C	0%
Potassium	7%	Folate	35%
Calcium	4%	Iron	13%

* Percent Daily Values are based on a 2,000 calorie diet. Your Daily Values may be higher or lower depending on your calorie needs.

This food was originally developed from wild plant species by people in this part of the world: **Western Asia**

Seed Food Name:
SUNFLOWER SEED (hulled)
Semilla de Girasol

Nutrition Facts

Serving Size	1/2 cup, dry roasted

Amount Per Serving

Calories	186

% Daily Value*

Total Fat	32 g	
Saturated Fat	3 g	
Cholesterol	0 mg	
Sodium	2 mg	
Total Carbohydrate	15 g	
Dietary Fiber	7 g	28%
Sugars	1 g	
Protein	13 g	

Vitamin A	0%	Vitamin C	1%
Potassium	15%	Folate	38%
Calcium	2%	Iron	13%

* Percent Daily Values are based on a 2,000 calorie diet. Your Daily Values may be higher or lower depending on your calorie needs.

This food was originally developed from wild plant species by people in this part of the world: **North America**

Botany Background: Form and Function

Plants

The most important and amazing characteristic of plants is that they make their own food using a process known as photosynthesis. Scientists are still studying the intricate nature of this complex process that supports most life on earth. (Some primitive plants and bacteria use a different process to capture energy.) Most plants have a green pigment called chlorophyll, which traps light energy. Green plants serve directly or indirectly as the source of food and support for animals and human societies. Coal, oil, and natural gas are the remains of ancient fern forests that used photosynthesis to convert light energy into plant matter.

Like animals, plants are composed of three-dimensional microscopic cells. Unlike animal cells, plant cells have rigid cell walls made mostly of cellulose. Cells that are actively dividing, growing, and producing new tissue are termed meristems. They are responsible for the increase in length of plant parts and are

Photosynthesis

fruit-stored sugar

light energy from sun

H_2O (water vapor)

CO_2 (carbon dioxide)

O_2 (oxygen)

Photosynthesis and respiration

sugars

water

sugar

soil line

tuber (storage)

starch

H_2O (water)

O_2 (oxygen)

minerals

water

CO_2 (carbon dioxide)

Respiration in roots

typically found in root tips, shoot tips, and the buds of leaves and flowers. The increase in stem and root diameter is due to the growth of meristems called cambium.

Although leaves are the main location for photosynthesis, a great variety of plant structures contain chlorophyll for converting light energy to make food. Photosynthesis begins when light reacts with chlorophyll in the cells, causing the splitting of water molecules (H_2O). Electrons from the hydrogen molecules are used to form energy storage molecules, and oxygen is released.

Carbon dioxide molecules, extracted from the air, are transformed into carbohydrates (sugar, starch, cellulose) using the hydrogen and the energy that was released by the breakdown of water. The chemical equation that describes photosynthesis is:

$$6CO_2 + 6H_2O \longrightarrow C_6H_{12}O_6 + 6O_2$$

Water plays a vital role in photosynthesis in several ways. First, water pressure is needed in plant cells to maintain shape and ensure cell growth. Second, water is split into hydrogen and oxygen by the energy of the sun that has been absorbed by the chlorophyll. The oxygen is released into the atmosphere and the hydrogen is used in manufacturing carbohydrates. Third, water dissolves mineral nutrients from the soil and transports them up from the roots and throughout the plant, where they serve as raw materials in the production of new plant tissues.

Plants convert some of the sugars they make during photosynthesis into energy that is used in the process of building new plant tissues. <u>Respiration</u> is the chemical process by which carbohydrates (sugar and starch) are converted into energy. It is the reverse of photosynthesis. Unlike photosynthesis, respiration occurs day and night in all life forms and in all cells. In animals, lungs, gills, or other moist surfaces exchange oxygen and carbon dioxide between blood and the external environment. In plants, these gases diffuse in and out through openings in the plant's surfaces called stomata.

Flowering plants, which are the mainstay of our agricultural system, are divided into two major groups, monocotyledons and dicotyledons, based primarily on the structures of their seeds. Monocots, as they are called, include plants such as grasses, lilies, and onions. Their seeds have one cotyledon (seed leaf); their flower parts are in multiples of three; and their leaves have parallel veins. Dicots include plants like carrots, beans, and apple trees, and have seeds with two cotyledons. The flower parts of dicots are usually in multiples of four or five and the leaves have netted veins.

Roots

The main functions of roots are to absorb water and nutrients, anchor and support plants in the soil, and to serve as food storage organs. A primary root originates at the lower end of the embryo of a <u>seedling</u>. A taproot forms when the primary root continues to grow downward and becomes enlarged as it stores food. The taproots of carrots and parsnips are the principal edible part of these crops. A root tuber is a special structure of a root that also stores food for the plant. Sweet potatoes are such an example.

A fibrous root system is one in which the primary root ceases to elongate, leading to the development of numerous lateral roots. These then branch repeatedly and form the root system of the plant. In general, roots will penetrate much deeper in a loose, well-drained soil than in a heavy, compacted soil.

The root cap at the tip of the root is an area of cell division and growth. Behind it is the zone of elongation, in which cells increase

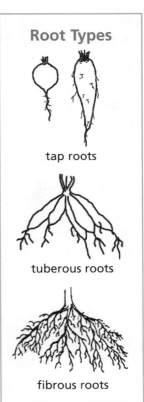

Root Types

tap roots

tuberous roots

fibrous roots

in size through food and water absorption. By increasing in size and number, these cells push the root through the soil. The outermost layer of cells is covered with minute root hairs that absorb water and nutrients. The center of the root contains tissues with tube-like structures (xylem and phloem) that conduct water and food. A continuous flowing column of water is maintained in the xylem as long as the pores in the leaves (stomata) are open and water is available in the soil. Roots possess a root cap, have no nodes, and do not directly bear leaves or flowers.

Stems

Stems are structures that support buds and leaves and serve as conduits for carrying water and nutrients. The three major internal parts of a stem are the xylem, phloem, and cambium. Xylem cells form tubes that conduct water and minerals from the roots to the top of the plant. Phloem cells conduct the carbohydrates produced in photosynthesis from the leaves to other parts of the plant. In the stem of a monocot, the xylem and phloem are paired into bundles, and these bundles are dispersed throughout the stem. In the stem of a dicot, the tubes are formed into concentric rings inside the stem. The ring of phloem is near the external cover of the stem and is a component of the bark in mature stems. The xylem forms the inner ring.

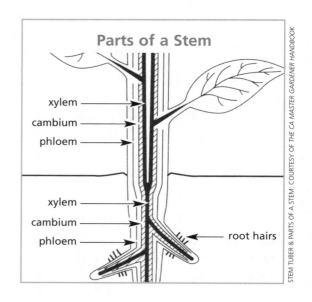

Parts of a Stem

xylem
cambium
phloem

xylem
cambium
phloem
root hairs

The cambium is an area of cell division and active growth located between the xylem and phloem in the root and stem. It produces both the xylem and phloem tissues and is responsible for the increase in diameter as the plant grows.

Nodes are areas of great cellular activity on the stem where buds develop into leaves or flowers. A bud is an undeveloped shoot from which embryonic leaves or flower parts arise. Stems may be long, with great distances between nodes (branches on trees and runners on strawberries), or compressed, with short distances between buds or leaves (dandelions).

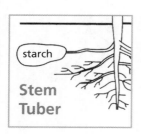

starch

Stem Tuber

A stem tuber is an enlarged extension of the stem that is underground, like white potato tubers, and that stores food for the plant. Like any other stem, the stem tuber has nodes that produce buds. The eyes of a potato are actually nodes on the stem. Each eye contains a cluster of buds, which can produce new stems and leaves. New roots develop from the new stems produced by the eyes (nodes).

Rhizomes are specialized stems that grow horizontally at or just below the soil surface. They also act as storage organs and means of propagation. Some rhizomes are compressed and fleshy such as those of ginger.

Rhizome Stem

Tulips, lilies, daffodils, and onions are monocots that produce <u>bulbs</u> — shortened, compressed, underground stems surrounded by fleshy scales (leaves) that envelop a central bud located at the tip of the stem. If you cut through the center of a tulip or daffodil bulb in November, you will see all the flower parts in miniature within the bulb.

It may sometimes be difficult to distinguish between roots and stems, but one sure way is to look for the presence of nodes. Stems have nodes, buds, or leaves; roots do not have these, but have root hairs. The edible portion of cultivated plants such as asparagus and kohlrabi is an enlarged succulent stem.

Leaves

The principal function of leaves is to absorb sunlight for the manufacturing of plant sugars in a process called photosynthesis. Many leaves develop a flattened surface in order to present a larger area for efficient absorption of light energy. Typically these leaves have many stomata (openings on their undersides) to enable transpiration of water and diffusion of gases in and out of the leaf.

Parts of a Leaf

leaf / blade / margin / midvein / petiole / bud / stem

Transpiration is the process by which a plant loses water, primarily through the openings in the leaf surface. This water loss is necessary for bringing in nutrients from the soil, cooling the plant through evaporation, transporting sugars and plant chemicals, and maintaining water pressure. The amount of water lost from the plant depends on several environmental factors such as temperature, humidity, and wind or air movement.

The leaf blade is composed of several layers. On the top and bottom is a layer of thickened epidermis. The outer epidermis in many plants has a waxy cuticle that protects the leaf from dehydration and diseases. The amount of wax increases with greater light intensity. For this reason, plants grown in the shade should be moved into full sunlight gradually over a period of a few weeks to allow the cuticle to increase and protect the leaves from sunscald.

Some epidermal cells are capable of opening and closing. Pairs of these "guard" cells regulate the passage of water, oxygen, and carbon dioxide through stomata in leaves. Conditions that would cause large water losses from plants (high temperature, low humidity) stimulate guard cells to close. Guard cells will also close in the absence of light. A large percentage of stomata occur in the lower epidermis (the underside) of leaves.

Photosynthesis occurs largely in the cells in the middle layer of the leaf, which contain green chloroplasts that hold chlorophyll. Simple sugars produced in the chloroplasts are converted to other sugars and starches (carbohydrates) that may be transported to the stems and roots for use or storage, or they may be used as building blocks for more complex structures, such as oils, pigments, proteins, and cell walls.

Leaves are supported away from the stem by stemlike appendages called petioles. Buds are

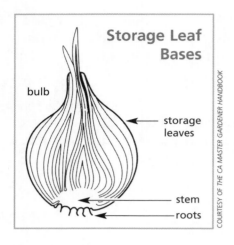

Storage Leaf Bases

bulb

storage leaves

stem

roots

located at the point where the petiole is attached to the stem at the node.

A number of rather distinct types of leaves occur on plants. Seed leaves, or cotyledons, are specialized leaves that provide energy for the sprouting embryonic plant. Spines and tendrils, as found on cacti and peas, are modified leaves that protect the plant or assist in supporting the stems. Storage leaves, as found in bulbous plants (garlic) and succulents, serve as food storage organs. Other specialized leaves include bracts, which are often brightly colored. The showy structures on dogwoods and poinsettias are bracts, not petals.

Leaf veins are the continuation of the phloem and xylem from the roots through the stems and petiole. In monocots, veins run parallel to each other the full length of the blade, connected laterally by minute, straight veins. In dicots, veins branch from the main midrib then subdivide into finer veins that unite in a complicated network. This system of enmeshed veins gives dicot leaves more resistance to tearing than most parallel-veined monocots.

The shape of the leaf blade and its edge is important in identifying species and varieties of horticultural plants. Simple leaves are those in which the leaf blade is a single continuous unit. A compound leaf is composed of several separate leaflets arising from the same petiole. The edge of the leaf, or leaf margin, is also a determining feature. Leaf margins can be smooth (entire), wavy (sinuate), toothed (serrate), and indented (lobed).

The various ways that leaves are arranged along a stem are also used to help identify plants. Opposite leaves are positioned across the stem from each other, two leaves at each node. Alternate or spiral leaves are arranged in alternate steps along the stem with only one leaf at each node. Whorled leaves are arranged in circles along the stem.

The leaf blade is the principal edible part of several agricultural crops, including collards, dandelions, kale, leaf lettuce, spinach, and Swiss chard. The edible part of leeks, onions, and fennel is a cluster of fleshy leaf bases. The petiole of the leaf is the edible product in celery and rhubarb. In plants such as brussels sprouts, cabbage, and iceberg lettuce, tightly clustered leaves form "heads."

Flowers

A flower's primary function is to attract pollinators. Its appearance and fragrance have evolved in part to attract animals, thereby ensuring sexual reproduction and the production of seeds. The parts of a flower include the male pollen, the female ovule, and accessory parts such as sepals, petals, and nectar glands.

Sepals are small green, leaflike structures at the base of the flower that protect the flower bud. Petals form the colorful corolla and may also be perfumed and contain nectar. The number of petals on a flower often helps to identify its plant family.

A plant's female parts are generally located in the center of the flower. Often shaped like a bowling pin, the pistil consists of the <u>stigma</u>, <u>style</u>, and ovary. The sticky stigma at the top of the pistil is supported by the style, which is connected to the ovary at the base. The ovary contains ovules, which, following fertilization, develop into seeds.

The stamen is the male reproductive organ. It consists of an <u>anther</u> (pollen sac) and a long supporting <u>filament</u> that holds the anther in position so the pollen may be dispersed by wind or carried to the stigma by insects, birds, bats, or other animals.

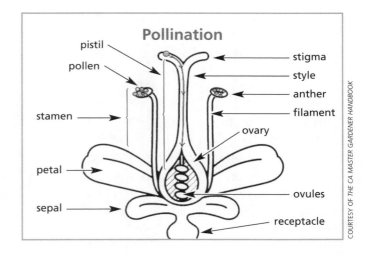

Pollination is the transfer of pollen from an anther to a stigma. This may occur by wind or by pollinators. Wind-pollinated flowers such as grasses lack showy floral parts and nectar since they don't need to attract a pollinator. Animal-pollinated flowers are brightly colored or patterned, fragrant, and/or contain nectar. In the process of searching for food or mates pollinators transfer pollen from flower to flower.

When pollen is deposited on the stigma, a chemical stimulates the pollen to grow a long tube down the inside of the style to the ovules inside the ovary. Sperm is released by the pollen grain and fertilization typically occurs. Fertilization is the union of the male sperm nucleus (from the pollen grain) and the female egg (in the ovule). If fertilization is successful, the ovule develops into a seed.

Cross-fertilization between plants combines different genetic material and generally produces stronger seed. The plant's reproductive success increases if its pollen is distributed beyond its own flowers to neighboring plants. Plants and their animal pollinators have coevolved an amazing array of strategies for improving the reproductive success of both partners.

If a flower has stamens, pistil, petals, and sepals, it is called a complete flower and it has the capacity to develop into a fruit. Tomatoes, strawberries, apples, pears, and peaches are species that bear complete flowers. If one component of a flower is missing, the flower is designated incomplete. Female flowers are incomplete because they possess a functional pistil but lack stamens; likewise, male flowers contain stamens but no pistil. Corn plants and pecan trees are examples of species that bear individual male and female flowers on the same plant. In some species, such as pistachios, there are separate male trees (bearing only male flowers) and female trees (bearing only female flowers). Only the female flowers bear fruits.

The largest family of flowering plants (*Asteraceae*) includes sunflowers and daisies that have "flower heads" composed of many individual flowers. These "composite flowers" frequently feature two types of flowers — ray flowers and disc flowers — displayed on a flattened receptacle, so that they appear to be one large flower. Ray flowers (usually infertile) form a ring around the inner disk flowers and have the "petal" structure. People native to the Americas cultivated sunflowers for the nutritious seeds produced by their disk flowers and for their enlarged roots, now known as sunchokes.

Broccoli is the most commercially important horticultural plant with edible flower parts. Artichokes are composite flowers cultivated for their edible receptacles and enlarged ray flowers. Nasturtium, violet, and pansy blossoms provide edible accents for salads and entrées.

Fruit

Fruit consists of the fertilized and mature ovules, called seeds, and the ovary wall, which may be fleshy, as in an apple, or dry and hard as in a peanut. The seeds are the only part of a fruit that is genetically representative of both male and female flowers. The rest of the fruit develops from the maternal plant, and is therefore genetically identical to that parent. Some fruits have seeds enclosed within the ovary (apples, peaches, oranges, squash, cucumbers). Others have seeds that are situated on the periphery of fruit tissue (corn, strawberries).

Fruits can be classified as simple, aggregate, or multiple. Simple fruits develop from a single ovary. Examples include cherries and peaches (drupe), pears and apples (pome), beans (pods), and tomatoes (berries). Some simple fruits are dry — the fruit wall becomes papery or leathery and hard. Peanuts (legumes), poppies (capsule), maple (samara), and walnuts (nut) are examples of these simple fruits.

Aggregate fruits, such as raspberries and strawberries, develop from a single flower with many ovaries. These fruits appear to have simple flowers, but each one has many pistils with ovaries. The ovaries are fertilized separately and independently. If ovules are not pollinated successfully the resulting fruits are misshapen and imperfect.

A multiple fruit is derived from a tight cluster of separate, independent flowers, borne on a single structure, that merge as the fruit develops. Pineapples and figs are examples of multiple fruits.

Seeds

A seed is made up of three parts: the embryo, stored food (cotyledon or <u>endosperm</u>), and seed coat. The embryo is a miniature plant in an arrested state of development. Most seeds contain a built-in food supply called the endosperm (orchids are an exception), made up of proteins, carbohydrates, oils, and fats. However, in some species a seed's cotyledons store food in place of its endosperm. A seed's hard outer covering is called the seed coat. It protects the seed from disease and insects, and prevents it from absorbing water (which initiates germination) too soon.

Germination is the resumption of active embryonic growth. Prior to any visual signs of growth

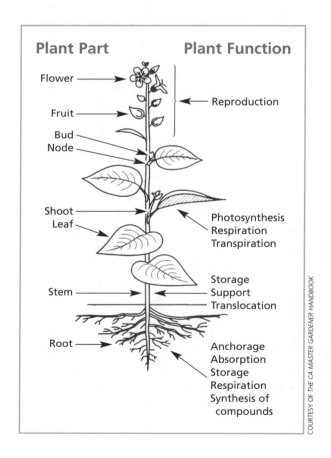

Plant Part — Plant Function

Flower

Fruit → Reproduction

Bud
Node

Shoot
Leaf

Photosynthesis
Respiration
Transpiration

Stem

Storage
Support
Translocation

Root

Anchorage
Absorption
Storage
Respiration
Synthesis of
compounds

COURTESY OF *THE CA MASTER GARDENER HANDBOOK*

the seed must absorb water. In addition, the seed must be exposed to proper environmental conditions — that is, oxygen, favorable temperatures, and for some seeds, correct light. Upon germination, the cotyledons become the seedling's first leaves. These "seed leaves" usually have a different shape than the leaves the growing plant will produce.

Plant Life Cycles

In horticulture, plants are grouped by the number of growing seasons required to complete a life cycle. Annuals are plants that pass through their entire life cycle from seed germination to seed production in one growing season and then die. Biennials are plants that start from seeds and produce vegetative structures and food storage organs the first season. During the second season flowers, fruit, and seeds develop to complete the life cycle. The plant then dies. Carrots, beets, cabbage, celery, and onions are biennial plants. Perennials are plants that, after reaching maturity, typically produce flowers and seeds each season and live for many years.

References

– *California Master Gardener Handbook*, Dennis Pittenger, Ed. (2002) by the Regents of the University of California, U.C. Agriculture and Natural Resources Publication 3382.

– *Master Gardner Manual* (1998) Cooperative Extension, College of Agriculture, University of Arizona, *http://ag.arizona.edu/pubs/garden/mg/botany.*

The Language of Science and Mathematics

The experiences in *Botany on Your Plate* offer children exciting things to talk and wonder about, along with new words for their growing understanding. The rich scientific content and vocabulary incorporated into the lessons' social learning process promotes language acquisition and oral and written communication skills.

A

absorb: to soak up liquid or gas.

adaptation: a characteristic of an organism that has emerged in a population of a species as a result of natural selection.

adapted: displaying characteristics that have been favored through natural selection, making the organism better suited for its environment.

allergy: hypersensitive reaction to environmental substances such as pollen, dust or microorganisms in amounts that do not affect most people.

analyze: to separate into parts or basic principles so as to determine the nature of the whole; to examine methodically.

anchor: to hold in place.

anther: the pollen-producing part of a stamen.

area: the amount of space inside a flat shape; measured in square units (e.g., square feet).

attribute: a quality or characteristic belonging to an organism or thing; a distinctive feature.

B

bee guides: patterns and designs on flower petals and sepals that lead to the nectar and/or pollen.

bisect: to cut lengthwise into equal halves.

blade: the flattened part of the leaf designed to capture light energy to make food.

botany: the study of plants.

botanist: a person who studies plants.

bred: the past tense of to breed; in this case, growers selected parent plants for specific genetic traits that would be exhibited in their offspring.

bulb: a collection of fleshy, food-storage leaf bases attached to a short, flattened stem, such as garlic.

C

carbon dioxide (CO$_2$): a molecule composed of one carbon atom and two oxygen atoms, used by plants in photosynthesis; a gas released in the process of plant and animal respiration.

carbohydrate: the principal food-storage substance of higher plants; may take the form of sugar, starch, or cellulose in plants;

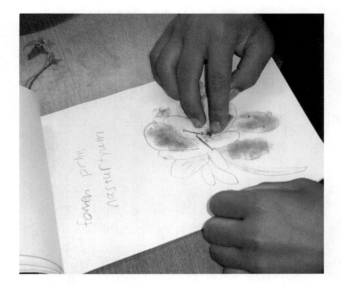

a source of food energy for plants, humans, and other animals.

cell: the smallest structural unit of living matter capable of functioning independently from which plants and animals are constructed.

characteristic: a distinctive quality that is typical of an object or organism.

chromatography: separation of a complex mixture by absorption through a selective filtering medium, yielding distinct layers.

chlorophyll: a green plant pigment located in chloroplasts of plant cells that captures the sun's energy. It is formed only in the presence of light, and enables the plant to make food during the process of photosynthesis.

compost: decomposed plant matter that when added to soil provides nutrients and structure; a recycling of organic waste.

conclusion: the closing statement(s) of a report providing an explanation of the results based on evidence from observations.

cotyledons: special leaves contained in the seed (for storing food for the embryo in some plants), that become the first leaves of a sprouted plant before true leaves develop.

D

data: measurements or observations used as a basis for reasoning, discussion, or calculation.

diagram: a plan, sketch, drawing or outline designed to explain something or clarify the relationship between the parts of a whole.

dicots: short for dicotyledons; plants distinguished by having two seed leaves, flower parts in fours and fives, and netted veins in leaves. Beans and fruit trees are examples.

diversity: degree of variation within a kind, for instance the number of different species of a plant or animal.

dissect: to cut something into parts to look carefully at its structures.

document: to record an observation in a systematic way.

E

effect: (noun) the result or consequence of an action or influence, as in: "the effect of sunlight on plant growth."

egg: a female sex cell.

embryo: an immature plant within a seed; the developing baby plant.

endosperm: food-storage tissue in seeds.

estimate: to make a judgment as to the approximate quantity of something.

evidence: the data on which a judgment or conclusion may be based, or by which proof of probability may be established.

explanation: the act or process of giving reason for or cause of an observable factor or event.

F

fertilization: the union of the male pollen cell and the female egg.

fibrous root: a thin root that is part of a highly branched, spreading root system.

filament: the stalk of a stamen, bearing an anther.

flower: a reproductive plant structure that has a pistil and/or stamens.

fruit: a mature ovary of a flowering plant that contains and protects the seeds.

G

germination: the beginning of growth of a seed, spore, or pollen grain.

H

horizontal: parallel to or in the plane of the horizon.

hypothesis: a testable explanation (if-then statement) based on observation, experience, or scientific reasoning including the expected cause and effect in a given circumstance or situation (hypotheses is plural).

I

investigate: to study by close examination and systematic inquiry.

J

journal: a record of observations, experiences, and reflections.

L

leaf: a plant structure that grows out from a stem and is the principal organ of photosynthesis in most green plants.

M

microscopic: too small to be seen by the unaided eye (i.e., without a microscope).

minerals: naturally occurring inorganic substances, such as iron and copper. These are absorbed by plant roots and combine with water in the stem, contributing to the health of the plant.

monocot: short for monocotyledons; plants distinguished by having one seed leaf, flower parts in threes, and parallel veins in leaves. Lilies and corn are examples.

N

nectar: a sugary liquid produced by some flowers to attract pollinators.

nutrients: substances that support plant and animal growth.

node: the location on a stem where primary growth can be initiated resulting in a bud that can grow into a stem, leaf or flower.

nut: a dry fruit with a hard ovary wall and usually one seed inside. May also have a fleshy outer fruit skin, like the walnut.

O

observe: to gather information and direct evidence by using the senses, often with the aid of scientific instruments.

observation: the act of noticing and recording a phenomenon, characteristic, or result.

ovary: the female reproductive part; in plants it is found at the base of the flower pistil and contains the ovules.

ovule: the plant structure containing an immature egg that when fertilized becomes a seed.

oxygen (O$_2$): an elemental gas that, as a molecule, is composed of two oxygen atoms; it is produced in the process of photosynthesis and consumed in the process of plant and animal respiration.

P

pattern: a consistent or repetitive set of data or observations where relationships can be observed, deduced, or inferred.

petal: the showy part of most flowers; they attract pollinators.

perimeter: the distance around a closed shape; a linear measurement.

petiole: the stalk of the leaf that attaches the leaf blade to the stem.

phloem: living plant cells that form tubes to transport food, produced during photosynthesis, to the rest of the plant.

photosynthesis: the plant process of making food — chlorophyll captures sunlight energy to power the conversion of carbon dioxide and water into sugars (food). The process also releases oxygen.

pistil: the female reproductive structure of a flower that includes the stigma, style, and ovary.

pod: a fruit in the form of a casing containing seeds, such as a pea pod.

pollen: a plant's male reproductive cells produced by the flower anther.

pollinate: (pollination) to move pollen from a flower stamen to a stigma usually by wind or an animal visitor (pollinator).

pollinator: an animal such as an insect (fly, beetle, bee, butterfly, moth), bird (hummingbird), or bat that moves pollen from one flower to another.

predict: (prediction) to state what may happen in an investigation based on prior knowledge and/or evidence from previous investigations.

R

range (of data): is the difference between the greatest number and the least number in a set of numbers.

reproduce: to make a new plant or animal, as in a parent producing offspring.

respiration (cellular): the process of releasing the stored energy in food to enable the processes of growth, repair, and reproduction.

root: part of a plant, normally underground, that absorbs water and nutrients and anchors the plant.

root hairs: extremely small lateral growths of the root that absorb water and nutrients.

S

seed: a reproductive structure formed from the maturation of an ovule, containing an embryo and stored food surrounded by a seed coat.

seed coat: the protective outer layer of a seed.

seedling: a young plant grown from a seed.

sepal: a flower part that encloses and protects the flower bud.

shoot: new plant growth, usually referring to the stem, that includes growing tips (buds) of leaves and/or flowers.

stamen: the male part of a flower consisting of an anther and filament.

stem: the part of a plant that transports water, nutrients, and food, usually extending above ground toward sunlight, that supports leaves and flowers.

stigma: the part of a pistil that receives pollen.

style: the narrow part of a pistil that connects the stigma and the ovary.

taproot: a prominent vertical root with few branches, usually swollen to store food; is a good anchor and is able to absorb water from deep underground.

true statement: an observation supported by evidence or one that can be made after evaluation of the data collected (may be mathematical).

tuber: a fleshy (usually thick and starchy) underground part of a plant in which food is stored. It may be a stem (e.g., potato) or a root (e.g., sweet potato).

vegetable: a cooking term for edible parts of plants.

Venn diagram: a way to compare two or more things by grouping characteristics.

vein: a tubular structure that transports water and nutrients in a leaf blade.

vertical: at a right angle to the horizon.

vitamin: substance found in foods, especially fruits and vegetables, which can serve a function in the human body for good health.

water (H_2O): a molecule composed of two hydrogen atoms and one oxygen atom; a substance that is essential to plants, animals, and all known forms of life.

xylem: water-conducting cells of plants forming tube-like structures from the roots to the leaves and flowers, and throughout the plant.